Vocabulary Builder: Words With Multiple Meanings

Levels 5–6
English

Rebecca Lamb

First edition 2013

ISBN 978-981-07-3088-8

Welcome to studySMÄRT !

Vocabulary Builder: Words With Multiple Meanings provides your child with opportunities to expand his vocabulary while developing his ability to comprehend what he reads.

Students frequently encounter words in the English language that have more than one meaning and are often confused by the multiple meanings of words. As your child gains greater exposure to vocabulary in relevant contexts, he is more likely to learn the meanings and strengthen his reading comprehension across context areas.

Each two-page spread targets a different word and invites your child to both read and understand the different meanings of the word, as well as to apply them in sentence construction.

How to use this book

1. Introduce the meanings of the word in the grey box at the top of the page to your child.

2. Let your child complete the exercises to match the use of the word to its correct definition. Direct your child to the Dictionary section at the end of the book to find other definitions of each word.

3. Direct your child to refer to the definitions given in the grey box at the beginning of each two-page spread to decide which definition is used in the pictures. Alternatively, expand your child's ability to think critically by getting him to think about which definition suits which occupation the most.

4. Let your child complete matching the sentences, taking time to direct him to the correct definition of the word used in each sentence if he encounters problems.

5. Reinforce your child's learning with an extension activity from page 113. These activities provide additional practice, and improve fluency and comprehension.

Note: To avoid the awkward 'he or she' construction, the pronouns on this page and page 113 will refer to the male gender.

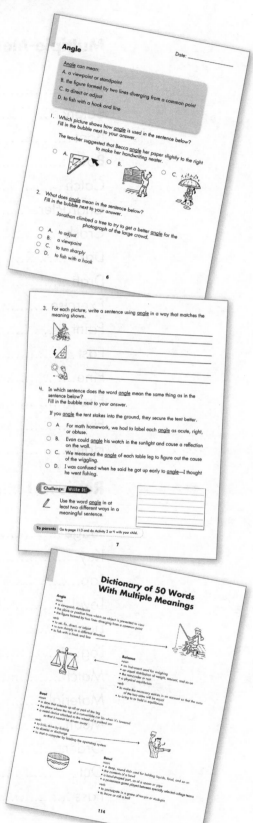

3

Contents

Multiple-Meaning Word Activities

Angle

Angle can mean:

A. a viewpoint or standpoint

B. the figure formed by two lines diverging from a common point

C. to direct or adjust

D. to fish with a hook and line

1. Which picture shows how <u>angle</u> is used in the sentence below?
   Fill in the bubble next to your answer.

   The teacher suggested that Becca <u>angle</u> her paper slightly to the right to make her handwriting neater.

   ○ A. 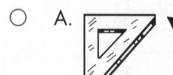   ○ B.    ○ C.

2. What does <u>angle</u> mean in the sentence below?
   Fill in the bubble next to your answer.

   Jonathan climbed a tree to try to get a better <u>angle</u> for the photograph of the large crowd.

   ○ A.   to adjust

   ○ B.   a viewpoint

   ○ C.   to turn sharply

   ○ D.   to fish with a hook

3. For each picture, write a sentence using <u>angle</u> in a way that matches the meaning shown.

_____
_____

_____
_____

_____
_____

4. In which sentence does the word <u>angle</u> mean the same thing as in the sentence below?
Fill in the bubble next to your answer.

If you <u>angle</u> the tent stakes into the ground, they secure the tent better.

○ A.   For math homework, we had to label each <u>angle</u> as acute, right, or obtuse.

○ B.   Evan could <u>angle</u> his watch in the sunlight and cause a reflection on the wall.

○ C.   We measured the <u>angle</u> of each table leg to figure out the cause of the wiggling.

○ D.   I was confused when he said he got up early to <u>angle</u>—I thought he went fishing.

Challenge: Write It!

Use the word <u>angle</u> in at least two different ways in a meaningful sentence.

_____
_____
_____
_____
_____

To parents   Go to page 113 and do Activity 3 or 4 with your child.

7

Balance

Balance can mean:

A. an instrument used for weighing

B. an equal distribution of weight, amount and so on

C. the remainder

D. to hold in equilibrium

1. Which picture shows how <u>balance</u> is used in the sentence below?
   Fill in the bubble next to your answer.

   The juggler could <u>balance</u> a bowling pin on his nose and still juggle 3 balls.

   ○ A.    ○ B.    ○ C.

2. What does <u>balance</u> mean in the sentence below?
   Fill in the bubble next to your answer.

   The charity spent most of the funds on new computers, and the <u>balance</u> on playground equipment.

   ○   A.   to make equal
   ○   B.   an equal distribution
   ○   C.   the remainder or rest
   ○   D.   the ability to stand steady

3. For each picture, write a sentence using <u>balance</u> in a way that matches the meaning shown.

_____
_____
_____
_____
_____
_____

4. In which sentence does the word <u>balance</u> mean the same thing as in the sentence below?
    Fill in the bubble next to your answer.

    After he bought new jeans, Derreck spent the <u>balance</u> of his allowance on video games.

    ○ A.   He started his homework at school, and did the <u>balance</u> at home.

    ○ B.   We had a contest to see who could <u>balance</u> the longest on one leg.

    ○ C.   Lucia learned how to <u>balance</u> a checkbook in her online math class.

    ○ D.   Emi used a <u>balance</u> to see whether her cell phone or video game weighed more.

    Challenge: **Draw It!**

    Draw a picture with a caption or a cartoon that illustrates how someone could confuse two definitions of the word <u>balance</u>.

To parents   Go to page 113 and do Activity 4 or 5 with your child.

9

Boot

> <u>Boot</u> can mean:
>
> A. to kick
>
> B. to start a computer
>
> C. a shoe that extends up the leg
>
> D. the place where a convertible car's top goes when it is put down

1. Which picture shows how <u>boot</u> is used in the sentence below?
   Fill in the bubble next to your answer.

   We all laughed at recess when Lauren's <u>boot</u> flew across the field
   as she kicked the ball.

   ○ A.    ○ B.    ○ C.

2. What does <u>boot</u> mean in the sentence below?
   Fill in the bubble next to your answer.

   The fullback on the soccer team could <u>boot</u> the ball all the
   way to the other end of the field.

   ○ A.   to start a computer
   ○ B.   to drive by kicking
   ○ C.   to dismiss or discharge
   ○ D.   a shoe that extends up the leg

3. Find the definition of <u>boot</u> that each person below would most likely use. Write the letter on the line.

_____ model   _____ programmer

_____ punter   _____ soccer player

_____ cobbler   _____ automobile dealer

4. In which sentence does the word <u>boot</u> mean the same thing as in the sentence below?
    Fill in the bubble next to your answer.

    Mr Herring's <u>boot</u> got stuck in the gutter as he
    climbed down from the roof.

    ○   A.   The convertible top slid off the top of the car and folded into the <u>boot</u>.

    ○   B.   The police put a <u>boot</u> on the illegally parked car, and the owner couldn't move it.

    ○   C.   The teacher told the students to <u>boot</u> up the computers as soon as they got into the lab.

    ○   D.   We had to search the house for Tasheka's left <u>boot</u> before we could play in the snow.

 Challenge: Write It!

Write a dialogue between two characters. Each person must use the word <u>boot</u> in a different way in a meaningful conversation.

To parents   Go to page 113 and do Activity 3 or 5 with your child.

Bowl

<u>Bowl</u> can mean:

A. a deep, round dish used for holding liquids, food, and so on

B. the contents of a bowl

C. to participate in a game of ten-pin

D. a bowl-shaped part, like of a spoon

1. Which picture shows how <u>bowl</u> is used in the sentence below?
    Fill in the bubble next to your answer.

    Sherlock Holmes tapped the tobacco down in the <u>bowl</u> of his pipe.

    ○ A.    ○ B.    ○ C.

2. What does <u>bowl</u> mean in the sentence below?
    Fill in the bubble next to your answer.

    Jaycob's grandmother always has a <u>bowl</u> of fruit on her kitchen table.

    ○ A.   a bowl-shaped part, like of a spoon
    ○ B.   the contents of a deep, round dish
    ○ C.   a deep, round dish for holding something
    ○ D.   to throw or roll a ball

3. For each picture, write a sentence using <u>bowl</u> in a way that matches the meaning shown.

_____

_____

_____

_____

_____

_____

4. In which sentence does the word <u>bowl</u> mean the same thing as in the sentence below?
Fill in the bubble next to your answer.

Rosita made sure there was a <u>bowl</u> for each guest to make a sundae.

○ A. Amy licked the peanut butter that stuck to the <u>bowl</u> of the spoon.

○ B. Sasha finished her slice of pizza just before her turn to <u>bowl</u> her last frame.

○ C. When they sat outside on the hot summer day, the <u>bowl</u> of ice cream melted quickly.

○ D. Elijah put his soup in a mug instead of a <u>bowl</u> to make it easier to carry to the table.

Challenge: **Write It!**

Write a dialogue between two characters. Each person must use the word <u>bowl</u> in a different way in a meaningful conversation.

To parents Go to page 113 and do Activity 3 or 4 with your child.

Catch

Catch can mean:

A. to trap or ensnare

B. anything that latches

C. to receive and take hold

D. to be in time to get aboard

1. Which picture shows how <u>catch</u> is used in the sentence below?
    Fill in the bubble next to your answer.

    The fishermen were particularly pleased with their <u>catch</u> yesterday.

    ○ A.    ○ B.    ○ C.

2. What does <u>catch</u> mean in the sentence below?
    Fill in the bubble next to your answer.

    My grandparents like to <u>catch</u> the early movie because it is
    usually less crowded.

    ○ A. to trap
    ○ B. to grasp
    ○ C. to attend
    ○ D. to be on time

3. Find the definition of <u>catch</u> that each person below would most likely use. Write the letter on the line.

_____ goalie   _____ exterminator

_____ hunter   _____ cabinet maker

_____ traveler   _____ train conductor

_____ carpenter

4. In which sentence does the word <u>catch</u> mean the same thing as in the sentence below?
Fill in the bubble next to your answer.

Colleen could not <u>catch</u> the frisbee with the sun shining in her eyes.

○ A. The softball was easy for Tara to <u>catch</u> with her new glove.

○ B. I had to run to <u>catch</u> the bus so I could get to school on time.

○ C. Luke and Ebony play <u>catch</u> with a football every day at recess.

○ D. They are hoping to <u>catch</u> a hockey game when they travel to Canada.

Challenge: Write It!

Use the word <u>catch</u> in at least two different ways in a meaningful sentence.

To parents Go to page 113 and do Activity 1 or 3 with your child.

15

Character

Character can mean:

A. a written symbol

B. a personality

C. a person in a play or work of fiction

D. integrity and force of personality

1. Which picture shows how <u>character</u> is used in the sentence below?
Fill in the bubble next to your answer.

   It was difficult to write the yearbook messages with a 50-<u>character</u> limit.

   ○ A. 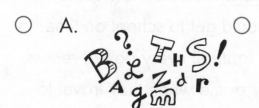   ○ B.    ○ C.

2. What does <u>character</u> mean in the sentence below?
Fill in the bubble next to your answer.

   The artifact found in the archeology dig had a strange
   <u>character</u> engraved on it.

   ○ A.   integrity

   ○ B.   a personality

   ○ C.   a written symbol

   ○ D.   an actor or actress

3. For each picture, write a sentence using <u>character</u> in a way that matches the meaning shown.

_____

_____

_____

_____

_____

_____

4. In which sentence does the word <u>character</u> mean the same thing as in the sentence below?
Fill in the bubble next to your answer.

A <u>character</u> from a popular cartoon was scheduled to be at the toy store today.

○ A. We had to identify at least three <u>character</u> traits for each person in the story.

○ B. The scientist found an unusual <u>character</u>, or letter, written on the ancient cave wall.

○ C. Julie will play a <u>character</u> who has her own band on the new show that starts tonight.

○ D. The lead played such a colorful <u>character</u> that we laughed throughout the entire movie.

Challenge: Draw It!

Draw a picture or cartoon with a caption or dialogue, illustrating how someone could confuse two definitions of the word <u>character</u>.

To parents Go to page 113 and do Activity 3 or 5 with your child.

Date: _____

Crash

Crash can mean:

A. a collision of automobiles, trains or other vehicles

B. to fall asleep

C. to break into pieces violently; shatter

D. Starched cotton fabric used to reinforce the spine of a bound book

1. Which picture shows how crash is used in the sentence below? Fill in the bubble next to your answer.

   You could hear the crash, or fabric, in the old book's binding cracking as Madelyn flipped through the pages.

   ○ A.    ○ B.    ○ C.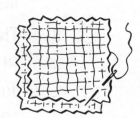

2. What does crash mean in the sentence below? Fill in the bubble next to your answer.

   Abigail knew she was in trouble as soon as she heard the vase crash on the ground after she threw the ball.

   ○ A. to shatter
   ○ B. to collide
   ○ C. a loud noise
   ○ D. a computer's sudden failure

18

3. For each picture, write a sentence using <u>crash</u> in a way that matches the meaning shown.

_____

_____

_____

_____

_____

_____

4. In which sentence does the word <u>crash</u> mean the same thing as in the sentence below?
Fill in the bubble next to your answer.

> Ella's brother loves to ride the bumper cars and <u>crash</u> into hers as much as possible.

○ A. The two cars involved in the <u>crash</u> had to be towed away to a repair shop.

○ B. After a long morning of chopping wood, Aiden came in to <u>crash</u> for a while.

○ C. When we do tricks on our bikes, my mother worries we might <u>crash</u> into one another.

○ D. The manager came running out of his office when he heard the loud <u>crash</u> in the store.

Challenge: Write It!

Use the word <u>crash</u> in at least two different ways in a meaningful sentence.

_____

_____

_____

_____

_____

To parents Go to page 113 and do Activity 1 or 5 with your child.

Dash

Dash can mean:

A. to move hurriedly

B. a footrace run at top speed

C. a small amount of an ingredient

D. a punctuation mark to set apart thoughts

1. Which picture shows how <u>dash</u> is used in the sentence below?
   Fill in the bubble next to your answer.

   Wyatt's grandfather likes to put a <u>dash</u> of cinnamon on his French toast.

   ○ A.    ○ B.    ○ C.

2. What does <u>dash</u> mean in the sentence below?
   Fill in the bubble next to your answer.

   The cook <u>dashed</u> off a pasta recipe for her cookbook.

   ○   A.   to do hastily
   ○   B.   a small quantity
   ○   C.   a hasty movement
   ○   D.   to rush

3. Find the definition of <u>dash</u> that each person below would most likely use. Write the letter on the line.

_____ chef   _____ courier

_____ baker   _____ sprinter

_____ editor   _____ author

4. In which sentence does the word <u>dash</u> mean the same thing as in the sentence below?
Fill in the bubble next to your answer.

> We watched the fox <u>dash</u> into the woods as soon as the dog ran across the field.

○ A. Zoe knocked the books to the floor with an impatient <u>dash</u> of her hand.

○ B. Nadia had to <u>dash</u> through the rain to try to keep her project from getting soaked.

○ C. Mason's mom said she would <u>dash</u> off a note to inquire about the upcoming field trip.

○ D. During his <u>dash</u> through the airport to catch his plane, Levi must have dropped his keys.

Challenge: Write It!

 Write a dialogue between two characters. Each person must use the word <u>dash</u> in a different way in a meaningful conversation.

To parents Go to page 113 and do Activity 1 or 5 with your child.

Draft

Draft can mean:

A. a first form of any writing, subject to revision

B. to draw up in written form; compose

C. a current of air in any enclosed space

D. to ride close behind another vehicle so as to benefit from the reduction in air pressure

1. Which picture shows how <u>draft</u> is used in the sentence below?
   Fill in the bubble next to your answer.

   The architect's <u>draft</u> of the new school building design was reviewed at the meeting.

   ○ A.  ○ B.  ○ C.

2. What does <u>draft</u> mean in the sentence below?
   Fill in the bubble next to your answer.

   Since it was time to go to practice, I saved the <u>draft</u> of my report to revise later.

   ○ A. a drawing, sketch, or design
   ○ B. a preliminary version
   ○ C. to compose or write
   ○ D. to draw the plan of

3. For each picture, write a sentence using <u>draft</u> in a way that matches the meaning shown.

_____

_____

_____

_____

_____

4. In which sentence does the word <u>draft</u> mean the same thing as in the sentence below?
Fill in the bubble next to your answer.

During language arts class, we had to <u>draft</u> a letter to our favorite author.

○ A.   Congress approved the final <u>draft</u> of the bill and hopes it becomes a law soon.

○ B.   We have to turn in a rough <u>draft</u> of our science research paper by next Monday.

○ C.   Paige stayed up late to <u>draft</u> her campaign speech for the student government elections.

○ D.   Jamal received an invitation to attend the <u>draft</u>, where he is likely to be a first-round pick.

Challenge: Draw It!

Draw a picture or cartoon with a caption or dialogue, illustrating how someone could confuse two definitions of the word <u>draft</u>.

To parents   Go to page 113 and do Activity 1 or 3 with your child.

Exercise

Exercise can mean:

A. a traditional ceremony

B. to exert muscles to keep fit

C. a musical composition played for practice

D. to make use of one's privileges or powers

1. Which picture shows how <u>exercise</u> is used in the sentence below? Fill in the bubble next to your answer.

Levi's trumpet tutor had him work on the same <u>exercise</u> for more than half an hour.

○ A.    ○ B.    ○ C.

2. What does <u>exercise</u> mean in the sentence below? Fill in the bubble next to your answer.

Each team member had to choose a different <u>exercise</u> for the players' warm-up.

○ A.   to exert muscles to keep fit

○ B.   to make use of one's privileges

○ C.   bodily exertion for the sake of training

○ D.   a written composition completed for practice

3. Find the definition of <u>exercise</u> that each person below would most likely use. Write the letter on the line.

_____ pianist   _____ body builder

_____ athlete   _____ band director

_____ gym teacher   _____ army general

_____ graduate

4. In which sentence does the word <u>exercise</u> mean the same thing as in the sentence below?
Fill in the bubble next to your answer.

Riley tries to do at least 30 minutes of <u>exercise</u> four times every week.

○ A. The football players had to <u>exercise</u> in the weight room three days a week.

○ B During the commencement <u>exercise</u>, the students will all receive their diplomas.

○ C. The <u>exercise</u> that the fencer did before his bout helped loosen and warm up his muscles.

○ D. Our language arts teacher told us to do the third vocabulary <u>exercise</u> for homework.

Challenge: Draw It!

Draw a picture with a caption or a cartoon that illustrates how someone could confuse two definitions of the word <u>exercise</u>.

To parents Go to page 113 and do Activity 3 or 4 with your child.

25

Date: _____

Faint

Faint can mean:

A. to collapse and temporarily lose consciousness

B. lacking clarity, loudness, brightness, or strength

C. feeling weak and dizzy

D. lacking courage

1. Which picture shows how <u>faint</u> is used in the sentence below?
   Fill in the bubble next to your answer.

   You could describe the lion in the *Wizard of Oz* as faint, or cowardly.

   ○ A.   ○ B.   ○ C.

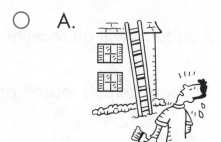      

2. What does <u>faint</u> mean in the sentence below?
   Fill in the bubble next to your answer.

   Callie was so nervous about speaking in front of the large crowd,
   she was afraid she would <u>faint</u>.

   ○ A.   cowardly; lacking courage

   ○ B   feeling weak and dizzy; about to pass out

   ○ C.   lacking clarity, loudness, brightness, or strength

   ○ D.   to collapse and temporarily lose consciousness

3. For each picture, write a sentence using <u>faint</u> in a way that matches the meaning shown.

_____

_____

_____

_____

_____

4. In which sentence does the word <u>faint</u> mean the same thing as in the sentence below?
Fill in the bubble next to your answer.

We could hear the <u>faint</u> sound of music coming from the concert two miles away.

○ A. The <u>faint</u> soldier was afraid to jump out of the plane with the paratroopers.

○ B. In the class play, Jayden has to pretend to <u>faint</u> when she hears she won a big prize.

○ C. The baseball players were shocked to see the umpire <u>faint</u> in the middle of the field.

○ D. The <u>faint</u> print on the old document was difficult to read, especially in the dim light.

Challenge: **Write It!**

Use the word <u>faint</u> in at least two different ways in a meaningful sentence.

_____
_____
_____
_____
_____
_____

To parents Go to page 113 and do Activity 3 or 5 with your child.

Fast

Fast can mean:

A. to give up food for a period of time

B. quick

C. indicating a time in advance of the correct time

D. soundly

1. Which picture shows how <u>fast</u> is used in the sentence below?
   Fill in the bubble next to your answer.

   Mrs Nelson was amazed at how <u>fast</u> the class finished the geometry quiz yesterday.

   ○ A. ○ B.  ○ C.

2. What does <u>fast</u> mean in the sentence below?
   Fill in the bubble next to your answer.

   The people in the crowd were on the edge of their seats during the <u>fast</u> race between the two sprinters.

   ○ A. loyal
   ○ B. quick
   ○ C. rapidly
   ○ D. soundly

3. For each picture, write a sentence using <u>fast</u> in a way that matches the meaning shown.

_____

_____

_____

_____

4. In which sentence does the word <u>fast</u> mean the same thing as in the sentence below?
Fill in the bubble next to your answer.

The <u>fast</u> horse was the favorite to win the race until he hurt his leg during warm-ups.

○ A. Madison ran as <u>fast</u> as she could to beat Avery in the 50-yard dash.

○ B. The <u>fast</u> flood waters carried the lawn furniture down the street.

○ C. The advertisement for the super glue said it would stick "hard and <u>fast</u>" to any surface.

○ D. Joyln described Carol as a <u>fast</u> and loyal friend that she had depended on for many years.

Challenge: Write It!

Write a dialogue between two characters. Each person must use the word <u>fast</u> in a different way in a meaningful conversation.

To parents Go to page 113 and do Activity 4 or 5 with your child.

Fine

> Fine can mean:
>
> A. healthy or well
>
> B. of superior quality
>
> C. delicate in texture
>
> D. a sum of money imposed as a penalty for an offense

1. Which picture shows how <u>fine</u> is used in the sentence below?
   Fill in the bubble next to your answer.

   Mrs Reed was very impressed with Delaney's dress of <u>fine</u> velvet.

   ○ A.    ○ B.    ○ C.

2. What does <u>fine</u> mean in the sentence below?
   Fill in the bubble next to your answer.

   Jeremy told his teacher he felt <u>fine</u>, even though he
   actually had a headache.

   ○ A. delicate in texture

   ○ B. healthy or well

   ○ C. of superior quality

   ○ D. in an excellent manner

3. Find the definition of <u>fine</u> that each person below would most likely use. Write the letter on the line.

_____ doctor   _____ hairstylist

_____ banker   _____ librarian

_____ jeweler   _____ parking attendant

4. In which sentence does the word <u>fine</u> mean the same thing as in the sentence below?
Fill in the bubble next to your answer.

> Cecilia had to pay a <u>fine</u> for the movie that she forgot to return to the video store.

○ A. The librarian said she would have to <u>fine</u> me for the lost book.

○ B. The <u>fine</u> for parking in front of a fire hydrant is $250 in Cypress City.

○ C. The paper in the old book was so <u>fine</u> you could almost see through it.

○ D. The <u>fine</u> thread was not strong enough to patch the hole in the seat cushion.

Challenge: Draw It!

Draw a picture with a caption or a cartoon that illustrates how someone could confuse two definitions of the word <u>fine</u>.

To parents   Go to page 113 and do Activity 1 or 2 with your child.

Fire

Fire can mean:

A. to ask rapidly

B. to bake in a kiln

C. to set off or launch

D. flames that give off light and heat

1. Which picture shows how <u>fire</u> is used in the sentence below?
   Fill in the bubble next to your answer.

   The Boy Scouts hope to <u>fire</u> their rockets in the park tomorrow afternoon.

   ○ A.    ○ B.    ○ C.

2. What does <u>fire</u> mean in the sentence below?
   Fill in the bubble next to your answer.

   The poet's voice was so full of <u>fire</u> as he read his latest work that
   we were all on the edge of our seats.

   ○ A.   great enthusiasm

   ○ B.   to ask rapidly

   ○ C.   to inspire someone

   ○ D.   flames or something burning

3. Find the definition of <u>fire</u> that each person below would most likely use. Write the letter on the line.

_____ firefighter

_____ potter

_____ lawyer

_____ clay artist

_____ police officer

_____ rocket scientist

_____ pyrotechnician

4. In which sentence does the word <u>fire</u> mean the same thing as in the sentence below?
Fill in the bubble next to your answer.

The forest <u>fire</u> burned uncontrollably for almost a week because of the windy weather.

○ A. The captain said he would have to <u>fire</u> Bobby if he was late to work again.

○ B. Raul put another log on the <u>fire</u> so he could roast marshmallows with his friends.

○ C. During basic training, the recruits will learn how to properly load and <u>fire</u> their guns.

○ D. The firefighters were able to quickly put out the <u>fire</u> before it caused too much damage.

Challenge: Write It!

Use the word <u>fire</u> in at least two different ways in a meaningful sentence.

To parents Go to page 113 and do Activity 4 or 5 with your child.

33

Fix

Fix can mean:

A. to repair or mend

B. to stare at an object steadily

C. a compulsively sought dose of something

D. to place definitely and permanently

1. Which picture shows how <u>fix</u> is used in the sentence below?
   Fill in the bubble next to your answer.

   My dad was able to <u>fix</u> the picture frame that I had accidentally broken.

   ○ A.    ○ B.    ○ C.

2. What does <u>fix</u> mean in the sentence below?
   Fill in the bubble next to your answer.

   Once we <u>fix</u> the decorations into position, the party can begin.

   ○ A. to place permanently
   ○ B. to repair or mend
   ○ C. to stare at an object
   ○ D. to arrange the outcome of

3. For each picture, write a sentence using <u>fix</u> in a way that matches the meaning shown.

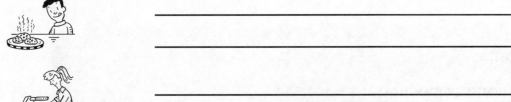

4. In which sentence does the word <u>fix</u> mean the same thing as in the sentence below?
Fill in the bubble next to your answer.

The plumber was able to <u>fix</u> the leaky shower in about ten minutes.

○ A. He always seemed to be able to <u>fix</u> the blame on someone else.

○ B. Sammie asked if his grandma would <u>fix</u> spaghetti when he visited.

○ C. Karl used super glue to <u>fix</u> the broken vase before his mom saw it.

○ D. I knew that I would be in a serious <u>fix</u> when my mom saw the broken lamp.

 Challenge: **Write It!**

Write a dialogue between two characters. Each person must use the word <u>fix</u> in a different way in a meaningful conversation.

To parents Go to page 113 and do Activity 3 or 5 with your child.

Hand

Hand can mean:

A. to give someone something

B. a round of applause

C. hired help for manual labor

D. the lower part of the human arm

1. Which picture shows how <u>hand</u> is used in the sentence below?
    Fill in the bubble next to your answer.

    Noah asked me to <u>hand</u> him the newspaper.

    ○ A.    ○ B.    ○ C.

2. What does <u>hand</u> mean in the sentence below?
    Fill in the bubble next to your answer.

    The teacher held the flash cards for the upcoming test in her <u>hand</u>.

    ○ A.   a style of handwriting
    ○ B.   the cards dealt to each player in a game
    ○ C.   the end of the human arm
    ○ D.   to give someone something

3. Find the definition of <u>hand</u> that each person below would most likely use. Write the letter on the line.

_____ factory owner   _____ ship's crew

_____ farmer   _____ member of a theater audience

_____ manicurist   _____ sign language interpreter

4. In which sentence does the word <u>hand</u> mean the same thing as in the sentence below?
Fill in the bubble next to your answer.

   I want to know who had a <u>hand</u> in this practical joke.

   ○ A.   My right <u>hand</u> hurt after writing for an hour.
   ○ B.   Cassandra had a <u>hand</u> in planning the surprise party.
   ○ C.   The talented piano player received a big <u>hand</u> for his solo.
   ○ D.   Mikey asked me to give him a <u>hand</u> moving the heavy furniture.

Challenge: Write It!

Use the word <u>hand</u> in at least two different ways in a meaningful sentence or short story.

_____
_____
_____
_____
_____

To parents   Go to page 113 and do Activity 1 or 4 with your child.

Review 1: Guess the Word!

Choose the word that best completes each pair of sentences. Fill in the bubble next to your answer.

1. The reporter's _____ on the story was different from those caught in the storm.

   My grandfather can estimate the time based on the _____ of the sun.

   ○ A. angle
   ○ B. balance
   ○ C. hand
   ○ D. catch

2. The customer was unhappy to get such a small _____ of soup.

   Murphy prefers to _____ with a ten-pin ball rather than a duck-pin ball.

   ○ A. catch
   ○ B. exercise
   ○ C. bowl
   ○ D. dash

3. Juan used a _____ to measure the chemicals for the experiment.

   The _____ in Camille's account was too little to buy the table she wanted.

   ○ A. catch
   ○ B. balance
   ○ C. bowl
   ○ D. draft

4. Luckily, no one was hurt in the car _____.

   Even though it was uncomfortable, Gavin was grateful to _____ on their couch after the long drive.

   ○ A. faint
   ○ B. crash
   ○ C. dash
   ○ D. fix

5. Toshi's computer had so many viruses that it would not _____ up.

   The officer threatened to _____ the recruit out of the platoon if he was disrespectful again.

   ○ A. fine
   ○ B. boot
   ○ C. fire
   ○ D. crash

6. The main _____ in the story searched for clues to solve the mystery.

   Since the ink was low in the printer, it was difficult to see every _____ in the words.

   - ○ A. fine
   - ○ B. character
   - ○ C. angle
   - ○ D. draft

7. On the last day of school, the class made a _____ for the exit as soon as the bell rang.

   I put a _____ of salt and pepper on my salad.

   - ○ A. dash
   - ○ B. crash
   - ○ C. fast
   - ○ D. fix

8. Sean ran fast and managed to _____ the ball.

   The tourists rushed to the station hoping to _____ the early train to the city.

   - ○ A. crash
   - ○ B. fire
   - ○ C. dash
   - ○ D. catch

9. Hayden was feeling _____ after working in the hot sun for two hours.

   As we pulled into the bakery's parking lot, there was a _____ smell of freshly baked cookies.

   - ○ A. fine
   - ○ B. balance
   - ○ C. dash
   - ○ D. faint

10. Diana had to _____ for twelve hours before the blood test to check her cholesterol.

    Tavon set his watch about ten minutes _____ to help him get to his appointment early.

    - ○ A. fast
    - ○ B. exercise
    - ○ C. faint
    - ○ D. fix

Judge

Judge can mean:

A. to rate contestants

B. a court official who decides legal cases

C. to conclude from evidence

D. to make a guess about; estimate

1. Which picture shows how <u>judge</u> is used in the sentence below?
   Fill in the bubble next to your answer.

   Lindsey was impressed that the <u>judge</u> had taken time to write comments about her essay entry.

   ○ A.    ○ B.    ○ C.

2. What does <u>judge</u> mean in the sentence below?
   Fill in the bubble next to your answer.

   The evaluator studied all the projects and was finally able to <u>judge</u> Camille's model to be the best.

   ○ A.   to rate entries in a contest
   ○ B.   to make a careful guess
   ○ C.   a person who selects the winner
   ○ D.   someone qualified to pass critical judgment

3. For each picture, write a sentence using <u>judge</u> in a way that matches the meaning shown.

_____

_____

_____

_____

_____

4. In which sentence does the word <u>judge</u> mean the same thing as in the sentence below?
Fill in the bubble next to your answer.

The <u>judge</u> asked Tony about the independent and dependent variables of his experiment.

○ A.   Each <u>judge</u> will rate the gymnast, and then all those scores will be averaged.

○ B.   To <u>judge</u> the pie contest, the chef inspected and tasted each entry several times.

○ C.   The <u>judge</u> was expected to deliver a verdict on the federal court case this morning.

○ D.   They were able to <u>judge</u> from the teacher's expression that she was pleased with their test results.

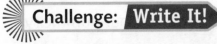

Challenge: Write It!

 Write a dialogue between two characters. Each person must use the word <u>judge</u> in a different way in a meaningful conversation.

To parents   Go to page 113 and do Activity 3 or 5 with your child.

Key

Key can mean:

A. to set text in type

B. important; essential; fundamental

C. tone or pitch

D. one of the levers in a musical instrument that sets in motion a playing mechanism

1. Which picture shows how <u>key</u> is used in the sentence below?
   Fill in the bubble next to your answer.

The scanner wasn't working so the cashier had to
<u>key</u> in a price for each item.

○ A.    ○ B.    ○ C.

2. What does <u>key</u> mean in the sentence below?
   Fill in the bubble next to your answer.

Only the <u>key</u> ideas from the passage should be included in your summary.

○ A. important, essential, fundamental
○ B. something that clarifies a problem
○ C. the principal tone of a composition
○ D. a systematic explanation of abbreviations

3. For each picture, write a sentence using <u>key</u> in a way that matches the meaning shown.

_____

_____

_____

_____

_____

_____

4. In which sentence does the word <u>key</u> mean the same thing as in the sentence below?
Fill in the bubble next to your answer.

The <u>key</u> with the crossword puzzle answers is in the back of the magazine.

○ A. The <u>key</u> to quickly completing the puzzle is to assemble all the edge pieces first.

○ B. Mr Saba grew anxious when he could not find the answer <u>key</u> to grade the tests.

○ C. Emily tried the <u>key</u> in all the doors but could not get it to open any of them.

○ D. Collin had to look at the <u>key</u> to figure out what all the symbols on the map represented.

Challenge: | Write It!

Use the word <u>key</u> in at least two different ways in a meaningful sentence or short story.

_____
_____
_____
_____
_____
_____

To parents Go to page 113 and do Activity 1 or 3 with your child.

43

Lap

Lap can mean:

A. the front part of the human body from the waist to the knees when in a sitting position

B. to move in small waves with a light slapping or splashing sound

C. to take in liquid with the tongue

D. to get a circuit or move ahead of a competitor in racing

1. Which picture shows how <u>lap</u> is used in the sentence below? Fill in the bubble next to your answer.

   The horse was so thirsty after the race that he trotted straight to the trough to <u>lap</u> up some water.

   ○ A.    ○ B.    ○ C.

2. What does <u>lap</u> mean in the sentence below? Fill in the bubble next to your answer.

   Josh wasn't running as fast as usual and knew his opponent would probably <u>lap</u> him before the end of the race.

   ○ A.   the complete circuit of a course
   ○ B.   to take liquid in with the tongue
   ○ C.   to move in small waves with a light slapping sound
   ○ D.   to get one track-length ahead of an opponent

3. For each picture, write a sentence using <u>lap</u> in a way that matches the meaning shown.

_____
_____

_____
_____

_____
_____

4. In which sentence does the word <u>lap</u> mean the same thing as in the sentence below?
Fill in the bubble next to your answer.

Doris prefers to race the 100-meter distance, which means swimming one full <u>lap</u> of the pool.

○ A.   After the second <u>lap</u> of the race, Marty was ahead of everyone by 60 feet.

○ B.   My aunt likes to sit on the beach and listen to the waves <u>lap</u> against the sand.

○ C.   Bianca sat on her mother's <u>lap</u> during the race so she could see the race better.

○ D.   Even though others were able to <u>lap</u> him, Leroy persevered and finished the long race.

Challenge: **Write It!**

Write a dialogue between two characters. Each person must use the word <u>lap</u> in a different way in a meaningful conversation.

To parents   Go to page 113 and do Activity 4 or 5 with your child.

45

Level

> Level can mean:
>
> A. to make a surface even or flat
>
> B. a story or floor of a building
>
> C. to talk frankly with
>
> D. filled to a height even with the rim of a container

1. Which picture shows how <u>level</u> is used in the sentence below?
   Fill in the bubble next to your answer.

   Nate's dad was glad the building had an elevator so he didn't have
   to carry the sofa to the sixth <u>level</u>.

   ○ A.  ○ B.  ○ C.

2. What does <u>level</u> mean in the sentence below?
   Fill in the bubble next to your answer.

   Margaret decided she was going to have to <u>level</u> with her grandmother
   and let her know she didn't like baby dolls anymore.

   ○ A. to make flat
   ○ B. relative rank or position
   ○ C. to knock down
   ○ D. to talk frankly with

3. For each picture, write a sentence using <u>level</u> in a way that matches the meaning shown.

_____

_____

_____

_____

_____

_____

4. In which sentence does the word <u>level</u> mean the same thing as in the sentence below?
Fill in the bubble next to your answer.

A wrecking ball will be used to <u>level</u> the old building and make room for a new playground.

○ A. Jeremy decided to <u>level</u> with his boss regarding his opinion of the building plan.

○ B. The construction worker used a bulldozer to <u>level</u> the dirt around the new house.

○ C. Conor used a <u>level</u> when he built the shelf on the wall to make sure it was straight.

○ D. Renee worked for hours on the card house only to have her brother <u>level</u> it with one blow.

Challenge: Draw It!

Draw a picture with a caption or a cartoon that illustrates how someone could confuse two definitions of the word <u>level</u>.

To parents   Go to page 113 and do Activity 1 or 2 with your child.

47

Line

Line can mean:

A. a row of written or printed letters, words, or text on a page

B. to mark with a line or lines

C. people, animals, or things standing one behind the other

D. to cover the inner surface of

1. Which picture shows how <u>line</u> is used in the sentence below?
   Fill in the bubble next to your answer.

   The geese seemed to fly in a perfect <u>line</u>.

   ○ A.    ○ B.    ○ C.

2. What does <u>line</u> mean in the sentence below?
   Fill in the bubble next to your answer.

   We had to <u>line</u> the beaker with foil before conducting the experiment.

   ○ A.   to mark with a line or lines
   ○ B.   a series of connected points
   ○ C.   to cover the inner surface of
   ○ D.   to form a line or border along

3. For each picture, write a sentence using <u>line</u> in a way that matches the meaning shown.

_____

_____

_____

_____

_____

4. In which sentence does the word <u>line</u> mean the same thing as in the sentence below?
Fill in the bubble next to your answer.

> When I saw the checkout <u>line</u>, I was glad I couldn't find what
> I wanted at the store.

○ A.   For homework, we had to illustrate and analyze one <u>line</u> of the famous poem.

○ B.   The <u>line</u> of people waiting to get tickets at the movie theater was unbelievably long.

○ C.   Mrs Ragan said we had to <u>line</u> the tin with waxed paper before we put the cookies in it.

○ D.   The telephone <u>line</u> was disconnected during the violent thunderstorm we had last night.

Challenge: Write It!

Use the word <u>line</u> in at least two different ways in a meaningful sentence or short story.

_____
_____
_____
_____
_____
_____

To parents   Go to page 113 and do Activity 1 or 4 with your child.

Log

Log can mean:

A. a small section of a tree trunk or branch

B. a journal or diary

C. to cut down, trim, and haul timber

D. to enter identifying data into a computer system to be able to use it

1. Which picture shows how <u>log</u> is used in the sentence below?
   Fill in the bubble next to your answer.

   The workers hope to <u>log</u> the entire pine forest by the end of the month.

   ○ A.  ○ B.  ○ C.

2. What does <u>log</u> mean in the sentence below?
   Fill in the bubble next to your answer.

   Bonnie had a difficult time splitting the <u>log</u> with the heavy ax.

   ○ A.   a record of observations or data
   ○ B.   to cut down, trim, and haul timber
   ○ C.   to cut tree branches into small sections
   ○ D.   a small section of a tree trunk or branch

50

3. For each picture, write a sentence using <u>log</u> in a way that matches the meaning shown.

_____
_____

_____
_____

_____
_____

4. In which sentence does the word <u>log</u> mean the same thing as in the sentence below?
Fill in the bubble next to your answer.

Julie panicked when she lost the <u>log</u> of data for her science fair project.

○ A. The scientist was careful to <u>log</u> data from the experiment accurately for each trial.

○ B. The captain kept a <u>log</u> of the daily adventures the crew had during the two-week cruise.

○ C. The first thing the students did when they went to the lab was to <u>log</u> on to the computers.

○ D. Steve needs to <u>log</u> 50 more hours with his instructor before he can get his pilot's license.

Challenge: Write It!

Use the word <u>log</u> in at least two different ways in a meaningful sentence or short story.

_____
_____
_____
_____
_____

To parents Go to page 113 and do Activity 3 or 5 with your child.

Match

Match can mean:

A. a small stick from which fire is struck

B. a pair of like items or people

C. a game or contest in which two or more opponents compete

D. to do as well as

1. Which picture shows how <u>match</u> is used in the sentence below?
   Fill in the bubble next to your answer.

   For homework, we had to draw lines to <u>match</u> the problems on
   the left to the answers on the right

   ○ A.    ○ B.    ○ C.

2. What does <u>match</u> mean in the sentence below?
   Fill in the bubble next to your answer.

   Mike tried for over an hour to <u>match</u> John's score on the video game.

   ○ A. to be alike

   ○ B. to go well with

   ○ C. to do as well as

   ○ D. to put into competition

3. For each picture, write a sentence using <u>match</u> in a way that matches the meaning shown.

_____
_____
_____
_____
_____
_____

4. In which sentence does the word <u>match</u> mean the same thing as in the sentence below?
Fill in the bubble next to your answer.

The teacher asked the kindergartners to <u>match</u> each picture with its beginning sound.

○ A.   By the second round, the wrestler knew he had met his <u>match</u>.

○ B.   Samantha's green-striped shirt did not <u>match</u> her blue-and-orange-plaid skirt.

○ C.   As she sorted the pattern blocks, Kelsey had to <u>match</u> the shapes with each other.

○ D.   In the game Concentration, you have to turn over two cards that <u>match</u>, or are the same.

Challenge: Write It!

 Write a dialogue between two characters. Each person must use the word <u>match</u> in a different way in a meaningful conversation.

To parents Go to page 113 and do Activity 3 or 4 with your child.

Material

> <u>Material</u> can mean:
>
> A. cloth or fabric
>
> B. the tools needed to make or do something
>
> C. the substance of which a thing is made
>
> D. of relating to, or in the form of matter

1. Which picture shows how <u>material</u> is used in the sentence below?
    Fill in the bubble next to your answer.

    Steel was the main <u>material</u> used to construct the frame of
    the new office building.

    ○ A.    ○ B.    ○ C.

2. What does <u>material</u> mean in the sentence below?
    Fill in the bubble next to your answer.

    A bed, dresser, and desk are all <u>material</u> objects in his bedroom.

    ○   A.   of, relating to, or in the form of matter
    ○   B.   of substantial importance or consequence
    ○   C.   of or affecting the well-being of the body
    ○   D.   the substance of which a thing is made

3. For each picture, write a sentence using <u>material</u> in a way that matches the meaning shown.

_____

_____

_____

_____

_____

_____

4. In which sentence does the word <u>material</u> mean the same thing as in the sentence below?
Fill in the bubble next to your answer.

One <u>material</u> needed for their Native American art
project is birch tree bark.

○ A. One <u>material</u> that every student should have every day in school is a pencil.

○ B. The <u>material</u> Kelsey chose for her dress has a funky red-and-purple pattern.

○ C. The lawyer was disappointed when the <u>material</u> witness did not show up to testify.

○ D. Nylon is often used as a <u>material</u> for making the rope that rock climbers use.

Challenge: **Draw It!**

Draw a picture with a caption or a cartoon that illustrates how someone could confuse two definitions of the word <u>material</u>.

To parents Go to page 113 and do Activity 4 or 5 with your child.

Mean

> <u>Mean</u> can mean:
>
> A. the average of a set of numbers
>
> B. unkind; nasty
>
> C. skillful or impressive
>
> D. to signify

1. Which picture shows how <u>mean</u> is used in the sentence below?
   Fill in the bubble next to your answer.

   After the tournament, we calculated the <u>mean</u> score for the two teams.

   ○ A.      ○ B.      ○ C.   18, ⑯, 9, 21

2. What does <u>mean</u> mean in the sentence below?
   Fill in the bubble next to your answer.

   We asked Bob to cook dinner because he makes a <u>mean</u> pot of chili.

   ○ A.   to signify or define
   ○ B.   nasty or malicious
   ○ C.   skillful or impressive
   ○ D.   an arithmetic average

3. For each picture, write a sentence using <u>mean</u> in a way that matches the meaning shown.

$2+2+4+3+4=15$
$15 \div 5 = 3$

_____

_____

experiment
(ik sper a ment)
noun:
a test, used
to find out
or prove
something

_____

_____

_____

_____

4. In which sentence does the word <u>mean</u> mean the same thing as in the sentence below?
Fill in the bubble next to your answer.

The <u>mean</u> temperature for the month of June was 86 degrees.

○ A. We had to find the <u>mean</u>, or average, for a set of numbers in math class.

○ B. Sally was punished for being <u>mean</u> and teasing her brother this morning.

○ C. When you want a reader to know what you <u>mean</u>, you must write clearly.

○ D. To declare a winner, the coach had to calculate the <u>mean</u> score for each player.

Challenge: Write It!

 Write a dialogue between two characters. Each person must use the word <u>mean</u> in a different way in a meaningful conversation.

To parents Go to page 113 and do Activity 2 or 3 with your child.

Order

Order can mean:

A. an authoritative command

B. a request for items to be supplied

C. conformity or obedience to rules or laws

D. a portion of food in a restaurant

1. Which picture shows how <u>order</u> is used in the sentence below?
Fill in the bubble next to your answer.

   Ryan placed his <u>order</u> for a new baseball bat on the Internet since the local store did not have the kind he wanted in stock.

   ○ A.    ○ B.    ○ C.

2. What does <u>order</u> mean in the sentence below?
Fill in the bubble next to your answer.

   Cindy requested an extra <u>order</u> of breadsticks with her take-out spaghetti dinner.

   ○ A. an authoritative command
   ○ B. a portion of food in a restaurant
   ○ C. to make a request for something
   ○ D. a request for items to be supplied

3. Find the definition of <u>order</u> that each person below would most likely use. Write the letter on the line.

_____ coach   _____ sales clerk

_____ waiter   _____ drill sergeant

_____ soldier   _____ security guard

4. In which sentence does the word <u>order</u> mean the same thing as in the sentence below?
Fill in the bubble next to your answer.

The students lined up in <u>order</u> from shortest to tallest
for the class photograph.

○ A.   For math homework, the students had to <u>order</u> the fractions from least to greatest.

○ B.   The captain gave an <u>order</u> to the troops to prepare their quarters for an inspection.

○ C.   Words in the glossary are arranged in alphabetical <u>order</u> to make it easier to reference.

○ D.   It was difficult to restore <u>order</u> after the principal announced that school would be dismissed early.

Challenge: **Write It!**

Use the word <u>order</u> in at least two different ways in a meaningful sentence or short story.

_____
_____
_____
_____
_____

To parents   Go to page 113 and do Activity 3 or 5 with your child.

Out

Out can mean:

A. absent

B. not working

C. unconscious

D. the opposite of in

1. Which picture shows how <u>out</u> is used in the sentence below?
   Fill in the bubble next to your answer.

   Bill's books fell <u>out</u> of his backpack because he forgot to zip it.

   ○ A.    ○ B.    ○ C.

2. What does <u>out</u> mean in the sentence below?
   Fill in the bubble next to your answer.

   The blow to the boxer's head knocked him <u>out</u>, and he lost the fight.

   ○ A.   absent
   ○ B.   external
   ○ C.   exposed
   ○ D.   unconscious

3. Find the definition of <u>out</u> that each person below would most likely use. Write the letter on the line.

_____ boxer   _____ wrestler

_____ umpire   _____ repairperson

_____ student   _____ baseball player

4. In which sentence does the word <u>out</u> mean the same thing as in the sentence below?
Fill in the bubble next to your answer.

After he broke his wrist in the first round of the playoffs,
Colton was <u>out</u> for the rest of the series.

○   A.   Haley ran as fast as she could but still got tagged <u>out</u> at third base.

○   B.   The black rhino is an endangered species that is at risk of dying <u>out</u> in a few years.

○   C.   He hung his sweatshirt on the hook, hoping it would dry <u>out</u> before he had to leave.

○   D.   Garret was <u>out</u> for a week when he had chicken pox and had to make up a lot of work.

 Challenge: **Write It!**

Write a dialogue between two characters. Each person must use the word <u>out</u> in a different way in a meaningful conversation.

To parents   Go to page 113 and do Activity 1 or 2 with your child.

Pass

Pass can mean:

A. to complete successfully

B. the transfer of a ball or puck from one teammate to another

C. to allow to go through or beyond a gate or barrier

D. to go beyond; surpass

1. Which picture shows how <u>pass</u> is used in the sentence below?
    Fill in the bubble next to your answer.

    If you aren't paying attention, it is easy to <u>pass</u> the unmarked
    door to the office.

○ A.  ○ B.  ○ C.

2. What does <u>pass</u> mean in the sentence below?
    Fill in the bubble next to your answer.

    Our teacher told us to study our notes and practice problems so
    we could <u>pass</u> the math test.

    ○ A. to skip one's turn

    ○ B. to deliver or transfer

    ○ C. to score average or above

    ○ D. to qualify for the next level

3. For each picture, write a sentence using <u>pass</u> in a way that matches the meaning shown.

_____

_____

_____

_____

_____

_____

4. In which sentence does the word <u>pass</u> mean the same thing as in the sentence below?
Fill in the bubble next to your answer.

Carlos gave the conductor his <u>pass</u> so he could ride the train.

○ A.   The movie <u>pass</u> was for any weeknight showing of the new film.

○ B.   The coach told the quarterback to <u>pass</u> the football to the receiver.

○ C.   You will see her house if you look out the window as you <u>pass</u> the lake.

○ D.   Claire's teacher asked her to use a <u>pass</u> when she left class to visit the nurse.

Challenge: **Draw It!**

Draw a picture with a caption or a cartoon that illustrates how someone could confuse two definitions of the word <u>pass</u>.

To parents   Go to page 113 and do Activity 1 or 3 with your child.

63

Patch

Patch can mean:

A. a small plot of land

B. a piece of material placed over a hole to mend it

C. a small emblem sewn to clothing

D. to mend with a small piece of material

1. Which picture shows how <u>patch</u> is used in the sentence below?
    Fill in the bubble next to your answer.

    The farmer had to <u>patch</u> the fence in several places to
    keep the rabbits out of the garden.

○ A.    ○ B.    ○ C.

2. What does <u>patch</u> mean in the sentence below?
    Fill in the bubble next to your answer.

    Mario asked his mom to <u>patch</u> his ripped tent so bugs could not get in.

    ○ A.   to restore in a makeshift way
    ○ B.   to mend with small pieces of material
    ○ C.   a small emblem of cloth sewn on clothing
    ○ D.   a piece of material placed over a hole to mend it

3. Find the definition of <u>patch</u> that each person below would most likely use. Write the letter on the line.

_____ tailor

_____ scout

_____ soldier

_____ gardener

_____ seamstress

_____ farmer

4. In which sentence does the word <u>patch</u> mean the same thing as in the sentence below?
Fill in the bubble next to your answer.

When his bike got a flat tire, Dion put a <u>patch</u> on the tube and filled the tire with air again.

- ○ A. Sydney tried to <u>patch</u> the hole in the raft, but it still lost air.
- ○ B. After his surgery, my grandfather wore a <u>patch</u> over his eye for two weeks.
- ○ C. The mechanic said the <u>patch</u> on the radiator would probably only last a month or so.
- ○ D. The Girl Scouts got a <u>patch</u> for their uniform when they completed the service project.

Challenge: Draw It!

Draw a picture with a caption or a cartoon that illustrates how someone could confuse two definitions of the word <u>patch</u>.

To parents Go to page 113 and do Activity 4 or 5 with your child.

Pen

Pen can mean:

A. to draw with ink

B. to put down in writing

C. a small enclosure for animals

D. a writing instrument with ink

1. Which picture shows how <u>pen</u> is used in the sentence below?
    Fill in the bubble next to your answer.

    The farmer led all the cattle to the <u>pen</u>.

    ○ A.    ○ B.    ○ C.

2. What does <u>pen</u> mean in the sentence below?
    Fill in the bubble next to your answer.

    Ryan's dream inspired him to <u>pen</u> the poem that won the writing contest.

    ○ A.   to draw with ink
    ○ B.   to put down in writing
    ○ C.   a person's style of writing
    ○ D.   a writing instrument with ink

3. Find the definition of <u>pen</u> that each person below would most likely use. Write the letter on the line.

_____ poet   _____ rancher

_____ artist   _____ novelist

_____ farmer   _____ shepherd

4. In which sentence does the word <u>pen</u> mean the same thing as in the sentence below?
Fill in the bubble next to your answer.

> The artist at the amusement park used an ink <u>pen</u> to draw a caricature of Patrick.

○ A. Luckily the submarine was in the <u>pen</u>, or repair dock, during the storm.

○ B. Using pastels, the artist created an intricate drawing of a <u>pen</u>, or female swan.

○ C. For homework, the art students had to <u>pen</u> an essay about Van Gogh's painting style.

○ D. Mrs Moore insists that her students use a pencil instead of a <u>pen</u> for math homework.

Challenge: Write It!

Use the word <u>pen</u> in at least two different ways in a meaningful sentence or short story.

_____
_____
_____
_____
_____

To parents Go to page 113 and do Activity 3 or 5 with your child.

Place

> Place can mean:
>
> A. a particular area of space or spot
>
> B. the position in a numeral or series
>
> C. a house or dwelling
>
> D. to put in a particular position or location

1. Which picture shows how <u>place</u> is used in the sentence below?
    Fill in the bubble next to your answer.

    Phyllis was careful to <u>place</u> the fragile statue securely on the high shelf.

    ○ A.    ○ B.    ○ C.

2. What does <u>place</u> mean in the sentence below?
    Fill in the bubble next to your answer.

    For their drill, the students had to <u>place</u> the ten numbers in order
    from least to greatest.

    ○ A.   to rank or put in sequence

    ○ B.   to put in a particular position

    ○ C.   to appoint someone to a job

    ○ D.   to identify in a particular context

3. For each picture, write a sentence using <u>place</u> in a way that matches the meaning shown.

_____

_____

_____

_____

_____

_____

4. In which sentence does the word <u>place</u> mean the same thing as in the sentence below?
Fill in the bubble next to your answer.

Even though students do not have assigned seats, Craig sits in the same <u>place</u> every day.

○ A. Steve asked us to save him a <u>place</u> in the cafeteria since he might be late.

○ B. The police were able to <u>place</u> the suspect at the scene of the crime last week.

○ C. Tammie invited Amy over to her <u>place</u> to work on their language arts project.

○ D. For math homework, Dan had to identify the digit in the ones <u>place</u> in each number.

Challenge: Write It!

 Write a dialogue between two characters. Each person must use the word <u>place</u> in a different way in a meaningful conversation.

To parents Go to page 113 and do Activity 1 or 3 with your child.

Pocket

Pocket can mean:

A. a piece of fabric attached to a garment that forms a pouch

B. any of the pouches at the corners and sides of a pool table

C. a small, isolated, or protected area or group

D. to put into one's pocket

1. Which picture shows how pocket is used in the sentence below?
   Fill in the bubble next to your answer.

   My cousin was about to pocket my favorite toy car when I caught him.

   ○ A.    ○ B. 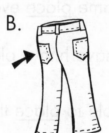   ○ C.

2. What does pocket mean in the sentence below?
   Fill in the bubble next to your answer.

   My grandfather always carries his watch in his pocket.

   ○ A. to put into one's pocket
   ○ B. small enough for carrying in a pocket
   ○ C. a piece of fabric on pants that forms a pouch
   ○ D. to continue

70

3. For each picture, write a sentence using <u>pocket</u> in a way that matches the meaning shown.

_____

_____

_____

_____

4. In which sentence does the word <u>pocket</u> mean the same thing as in the sentence below?
Fill in the bubble next to your answer.

The weatherperson said the <u>pocket</u> of clouds to the west could cause some brief showers during the game.

○ A. Shaun shoved his hands in his sweatshirt <u>pocket</u> to try to keep them warm.

○ B. Katie was surprised when the ball dropped in the right corner <u>pocket</u> of the pool table.

○ C. There was a small <u>pocket</u> of evergreen trees in the mostly deciduous forest.

○ D. The quarterback was forced out of the <u>pocket</u> and couldn't make a good throw.

⁂ Challenge: **Draw It!**

✏ Draw a picture with a caption or a cartoon that illustrates how someone could confuse two definitions of the word <u>pocket</u>.

To parents Go to page 113 and do Activity 1 or 2 with your child.

Review 2: Guess the Word!

Choose the word that best completes each pair of sentences. Fill in the bubble next to your answer.

1. Linda carefully held the birthday cake in her
    _____ so it wouldn't slide around in the
    car.

    Kathy likes to finish each workout at the pool
    with one _____ of the butterfly stroke.

    ○ A. hand
    ○ B. lap
    ○ C. bowl
    ○ D. press

2. Rob put another _____ on the campfire
    so it would keep burning a little longer.

    We had to keep a _____ of everything
    we ate for one week.

    ○ A. fire
    ○ B. draft
    ○ C. match
    ○ D. log

3. Kari's piano teacher insisted that both
    thumbs rest on the middle _____.

    Anne's manager asked her to note down
    the _____ points.

    ○ A. key
    ○ B. note
    ○ C. block
    ○ D. pocket

4. The milk was _____ with the rim of the
    glass so Owen took a sip before carrying it
    to the table.

    Caroline lives on the fourth _____ of
    the building.

    ○ A. balance
    ○ B. line
    ○ C. level
    ○ D. place

5. A warm house and nutritious food are
    _____ comforts that no one should
    live without.

    The seamstress ran out of _____ when
    she still had four costumes left to make.

    ○ A. order
    ○ B. character
    ○ C. place
    ○ D. material

6. The artist will study each of the sculptures and _____ them on originality and creativity.

○ A. place
○ B. order
○ C. judge
○ D. fan

The _____ listened patiently to all the witnesses.

7. The actor got so nervous he could not remember his next _____.

○ A. patch
○ B. line
○ C. material
○ D. order

Marc joined the long _____ at the cafeteria.

8. Chris gathered kindling and wood and then used a _____ to light the campfire.

○ A. exercise
○ B. match
○ C. line
○ D. fire

During the tennis _____, Karen beat her opponent by three sets.

9. "Please explain what you _____ when you say that", said the teacher.

○ A. fix
○ B. match
○ C. mean
○ D. faint

Chris was so _____ to his little brother that his mother reprimanded him.

10. The director was pleased that everything seemed to be in _____ for the opening night performance.

○ A. order
○ B. place
○ C. line
○ D. pocket

Colin plans to _____ flowers for his grandmother's birthday next month.

Point

Point can mean:

A. a sharp or tapering end

B. any definite position

C. a purpose or reason

D. to direct or aim

1. Which picture shows how <u>point</u> is used in the sentence below?
   Fill in the bubble next to your answer.

   To fill the balloon at the carnival game, you have to <u>point</u> the
   water gun at the clown's mouth.

   ○ A.  ○ B.  ○ C.

2. What does <u>point</u> mean in the sentence below?
   Fill in the bubble next to your answer.

   Clara did not understand the <u>point</u> of the assignment and had a
   difficult time completing it correctly.

   ○ A. to direct or aim

   ○ B. a purpose or reason

   ○ C. to show position of

   ○ D. a certain place or position

3. For each picture, write a sentence using <u>point</u> in a way that matches the meaning shown.

_____

_____

_____

_____

_____

_____

4. In which sentence does the word <u>point</u> mean the same thing as in the sentence below?
Fill in the bubble next to your answer.

> She uses a thimble when she quilts, so the <u>point</u> of the needle doesn't prick her.

○ A.   One of the test questions asked students to identify the author's <u>point</u> of view.

○ B.   Ricky prefers a sharp <u>point</u>, so he sharpened his pencil six times during the test.

○ C.   The hikers planned to reach the peak, or highest <u>point</u>, of the mountain in three days.

○ D.   Ron hurled the ball towards the goal at the last second and scored the winning <u>point</u>.

Challenge: **Write It!**

Use the word <u>point</u> in at least two different ways in a meaningful sentence or short story.

_____

_____

_____

_____

_____

To parents   Go to page 113 and do Activity 1 or 5 with your child.

75

Pound

Pound can mean:

A. a unit of weight

B. to strike with great force

C. to beat or throb, as the heart

D. a monetary unit in various countries

1. Which picture shows how <u>pound</u> is used in the sentence below?
Fill in the bubble next to your answer.

The butcher suggested that my mom <u>pound</u> the roast with a
meat tenderizer before cooking it.

○ A.    ○ B.    ○ C.

2. What does <u>pound</u> mean in the sentence below?
Fill in the bubble next to your answer.

From a mile away, you could feel the <u>pound</u> of the wrecking ball
destroying the building.

○ A.   to beat or throb

○ B.   to crush into a powder

○ C.   a heavy or forcible blow

○ D.   to strike with great force

76

3. Find the definition of <u>pound</u> that each person below would most likely use. Write the letter on the line.

_____ grocer   _____ carpenter

_____ banker   _____ Englishman

_____ dietician   _____ cardiologist

4. In which sentence does the word <u>pound</u> mean the same thing as in the sentence below?
Fill in the bubble next to your answer.

Corey bought a <u>pound</u> of grapes at the farmers market for only a dollar.

○ A. When she was in England, Tristana bought three apples from the grocer for a <u>pound</u>.

○ B. Jorge's brother used a mallet to <u>pound</u> the apple to pieces, hoping to make apple juice.

○ C. Aisha could feel her heart <u>pound</u> as she raced to catch her brother hiding in the orchard.

○ D. To make paste, we added cold water to one <u>pound</u> of flour and cooked it for five minutes.

 Challenge: Write It!

 Write a dialogue between two characters. Each person must use the word <u>pound</u> in a different way in a meaningful conversation.

To parents Go to page 113 and do Activity 1 or 5 with your child.

Prime

Prime can mean:

A. a high quality or grade

B. of the greatest relevance or significance

C. an integer evenly divisible only by itself and 1

D. to make ready; prepare

1. Which picture shows how <u>prime</u> is used in the sentence below?
   Fill in the bubble next to your answer.

   Before Daniel pulled the rope to start the lawn mower, he had to push a button to <u>prime</u> the engine.

   ◯ A.    ◯ B.    ◯ C.

2. What does <u>prime</u> mean in the sentence below?
   Fill in the bubble next to your answer.

   Her skinned knee is a <u>prime</u> example of why you should wear knee pads when skate boarding.

   ◯ A. to make ready
   ◯ B. of the greatest significance
   ◯ C. a state of great perfection
   ◯ D. a designation of high quality

3. Find the definition of <u>prime</u> that each person below would most likely use. Write the letter on the line.

_____ chef   _____ food inspector

_____ butcher   _____ mathematician

_____ mechanic   _____ algebra teacher

4. In which sentence does the word <u>prime</u> mean the same thing as in the sentence below?
Fill in the bubble next to your answer.

A <u>prime</u> choice at the new steak restaurant is the filet mignon.

○ A.   Brianna's mom fixed a <u>prime</u> rib for a special dinner last Saturday night.

○ B.   Cattle ranching is the <u>prime</u> cause of deforestation in the Brazilian Amazon.

○ C.   The <u>prime</u> meridian at 0 degrees longitude passes through Greenwich, England.

○ D.   The painter used white paint on the wall to <u>prime</u> it before applying blue paint.

Challenge: Draw It!

Draw a picture with a caption or a cartoon that illustrates how someone could confuse two definitions of the word <u>prime</u>.

To parents Go to page 113 and do Activity 1 or 2 with your child.

79

Range

Range can mean:

A. a place for aiming at targets with various projectiles

B. to roam or wander freely

C. the difference between the lowest and highest values

D. a stove with spaces for cooking several things at once

1. Which picture shows how <u>range</u> is used in the sentence below?
   Fill in the bubble next to your answer.

   The farmer could not help sneaking a taste of the soup he found simmering on the <u>range</u> in the kitchen.

   ○ A.    ○ B.    ○ C.

2. What does <u>range</u> mean in the sentence below?
   Fill in the bubble next to your answer.

   The scouts will have to <u>range</u> the woods to find a suitable place to set up their tents.

   ○ A.   to set in proper order

   ○ B.   to roam or wander freely

   ○ C.   a large tract of open land

   ○ D.   to vary within certain limits

3. Find the definition of <u>range</u> that each person below would most likely use. Write the letter on the line.

_____ chef   _____ caterer

_____ golfer   _____ statistician

_____ police   _____ mathematician

_____ archer

4. In which sentence does the word <u>range</u> mean the same thing as in the sentence below?
Fill in the bubble next to your answer.

   The age <u>range</u> between Michael and his older brother is fifteen years.

  ○   A.   Joe found that the video games for sale were available at a wide <u>range</u> of prices.

  ○   B.   Kim is always trying to widen the <u>range</u> of what she knows about other countries.

  ○   C.   The cowboys rounded up the cattle on the <u>range</u> and moved them to a corral for branding.

  ○   D.   The ages of the children attending the tennis camp this week <u>range</u> from eight to fourteen.

Challenge: Write It!

Use the word <u>range</u> in at least two different ways in a meaningful sentence or short story.

_____

_____

_____

_____

_____

To parents   Go to page 113 and do Activity 1 or 3 with your child.

Rate

Rate can mean:

A. a degree of speed

B. the cost per unit of service

C. to evaluate the performance of; judge the quality of

D. the amount of interest charged for a loan

1. Which picture shows how <u>rate</u> is used in the sentence below?
   Fill in the bubble next to your answer.

   Mrs Ragan asked Lenora what her <u>rate</u> would be for babysitting.

   ○ A.    ○ B.    ○ C.

2. What does <u>rate</u> mean in the sentence below?
   Fill in the bubble next to your answer.

   As we looked at the science projects, we used a rubric to <u>rate</u> each one.

   ○ A.   to judge the quality of
   ○ B.   to merit or deserve
   ○ C.   to estimate value of
   ○ D.   to place in a certain class

3. Find the definition of <u>rate</u> that each person below would most likely use.
    Write the letter on the line.

    _____ banker   _____ contest judge

    _____ babysitter   _____ race car driver

    _____ book critic   _____ marathon runner

4. In which sentence does the word <u>rate</u> mean the same thing as in the
    sentence below?
    Fill in the bubble next to your answer.

    During the audition, four judges will <u>rate</u> Abby's performance and
        decide if she can play with the prestigious orchestra.

    ○ A.   Even at his slow <u>rate</u> of speed, the tortoise was able to beat the
            hare.

    ○ B.   The teacher administered a fluency test to assess the student's
            accuracy and <u>rate</u>.

    ○ C.   Mr Walker used a five-star scale to <u>rate</u> each movie he critiqued
            for the newspaper.

    ○ D.   The Federal Reserve may decide to raise the interest <u>rate</u> after the
            good economic quarter.

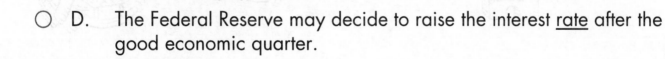

Challenge: Write It!

 Write a dialogue between two
characters. Each person must use
the word <u>rate</u> in a different way in a
meaningful conversation.

To parents   Go to page 113 and do Activity 1 or 3 with your child.

Rock

Rock can mean:

A. to shake violently

B. to play or dance to music

C. to sway back and forth gently

D. a large diamond or gemstone

1. Which picture shows how <u>rock</u> is used in the sentence below?
Fill in the bubble next to your answer.

My mom had to <u>rock</u> the crying baby to sleep.

○ A. 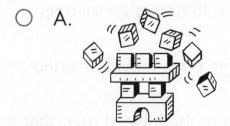   ○ B.    ○ C.

2. What does <u>rock</u> mean in the sentence below?
Fill in the bubble next to your answer.

The earthquake was enough to <u>rock</u> the train off its track.

○ A.   to cause to sway violently

○ B.   a firm foundation or support

○ C.   a fragment or piece of stone

○ D.   to move back and forth gently

3. Find the definition of <u>rock</u> that each person below would most likely use. Write the letter on the line.

_____ jeweler

_____ guitarist

_____ musician

_____ bride-to-be

_____ seismologist

_____ dancer

4. In which sentence does the word <u>rock</u> mean the same thing as in the sentence below?
Fill in the bubble next to your answer.

Every evening my grandmother likes to <u>rock</u> in her chair and knit.

○ A. Donna sat quietly in the car listening to <u>rock</u> music on her iPod.

○ B. The sailboat would <u>rock</u> back and forth each time a ship passed.

○ C. Kyle found a big white <u>rock</u> buried in the corner of the sandbox.

○ D. The jeweler used a jeweler's loupe to inspect the <u>rock</u> in her ring.

✸ Challenge: **Write It!** ➤

✎ Use the word <u>rock</u> in at least two different ways in a meaningful sentence or short story.

_____

_____

_____

_____

_____

To parents Go to page 113 and do Activity 4 or 5 with your child.

Run

Run can mean:

A. to operate

B. to flow

C. colors that bleed or spread

D. move at a fast pace on the feet

1. Which picture shows how <u>run</u> is used in the sentence below?
   Fill in the bubble next to your answer.

   Holly had to <u>run</u> to the poll so she could cast her vote
   before the election deadline.

   ○ A.    ○ B.    ○ C.

2. What does <u>run</u> mean in the sentence below?
   Fill in the bubble next to your answer.

   Terry learned to <u>run</u> the big tractor before he was allowed
   to dig up rocks in the quarry.

   ○ A.   to flow

   ○ B.   to operate

   ○ C.   to unravel

   ○ D.   to creep

3. Find the definition of <u>run</u> that each person below would most likely use. Write the letter on the line.

_____ artist

_____ plumber

_____ electrician

_____ dry cleaner

_____ marathon runner

_____ painter

4. In which sentence does the word <u>run</u> mean the same thing as in the sentence below?
Fill in the bubble next to your answer.

The electricity will <u>run</u> through the wires
until the power is turned off.

○ A. They will have to <u>run</u> if they want to get there before the show begins.

○ B. He finished the mile <u>run</u> in 6 minutes and 38 seconds to set a new school record.

○ C. Dad told Sasha that the water would <u>run</u> if she didn't turn the faucet off tightly.

○ D. Eddie decided to <u>run</u> for class president because he wanted to change some rules.

Challenge: Write It!

 Write a dialogue between two characters. Each person must use the word <u>run</u> in a different way in a meaningful conversation.

To parents Go to page 113 and do Activity 1 or 4 with your child.

Shape

> Shape can mean:
>
> A. an outline or contour
>
> B. to give definite form or character to; create
>
> C. the contour of a person's body
>
> D. to direct the course of

1. Which picture shows how __shape__ is used in the sentence below?
   Fill in the bubble next to your answer.

   A square is a flat __shape__ with four equal sides and four 90-degree angles.

   ○ A.    ○ B.    ○ C.

2. What does __shape__ mean in the sentence below?
   Fill in the bubble next to your answer.

   The mechanic heated the exhaust pipe in order to __shape__ it
   around the rear axle of the car.

   ○ A.   an outline or contour
   ○ B.   to direct the course of
   ○ C.   to give a definite form to
   ○ D.   an orderly arrangement

3. For each picture, write a sentence using <u>shape</u> in a way that matches the meaning shown.

_____

_____

_____

_____

_____

4. In which sentence does the word <u>shape</u> mean the same thing as in the sentence below?
Fill in the bubble next to your answer.

Once the glass was melted, the glass blower could <u>shape</u> the bulb ornaments.

○ A. Frank wanted to get into <u>shape</u> before the soccer season, so he started exercising.

○ B. Marty used tagboard to make the paper hats, hoping they would keep their <u>shape</u>.

○ C. From the <u>shape</u> the room was in, it was easy to tell a party had been held there.

○ D. The Japanese woman could <u>shape</u> the paper into origami figures in just a few seconds.

Challenge: Write It!

Use the word <u>shape</u> in at least two different ways in a meaningful sentence or short story.

_____

_____

_____

_____

_____

To parents   Go to page 113 and do Activity 4 or 5 with your child.

Shower

> Shower can mean:
>
> A. a brief fall of precipitation
>
> B. a party to give gifts to someone
>
> C. the stall in which a bath is taken
>
> D. a bath in which the water is sprayed from overhead

1. Which picture shows how <u>shower</u> is used in the sentence below?
   Fill in the bubble next to your answer.

   Her maid of honor threw Marissa a bridal <u>shower</u> before the wedding.

   ○ A.    ○ B.    ○ C.

2. What does <u>shower</u> mean in the sentence below?
   Fill in the bubble next to your answer.

   The contractor installed a new <u>shower</u> in the master bathroom.

   ○ A. an abundant flow or outpouring
   ○ B. the stall in which water sprays from overhead
   ○ C. a brief fall of precipitation, such as rain or snow
   ○ D. a bath in which water is sprayed from overhead

3. Find the definition of <u>shower</u> that each person below would most likely use. Write the letter on the line.

_____ housekeeper   _____ plumber

_____ bride   _____ weatherperson

_____ farmer   _____ expectant mother

4. In which sentence does the word <u>shower</u> mean the same thing as in the sentence below?
Fill in the bubble next to your answer.

My mom makes me take a <u>shower</u> every night before bed.

○ A.   The baseball game was delayed due to a short <u>shower</u>.

○ B.   My father called the plumber to help him fix our leaky <u>shower</u>.

○ C.   After playing a soccer game in the mud, Shane needed a <u>shower</u>.

○ D.   My little brother tried to <u>shower</u> me with spaghetti while we ate dinner.

 Challenge: Write It!

Write a dialogue between two characters. Each person must use the word <u>shower</u> in a different way in a meaningful conversation.

To parents   Go to page 113 and do Activity 3 or 5 with your child.

Slide

Slide can mean:

A. a small, flat piece of glass on which specimens are mounted for microscopic study

B. to glide or pass smoothly

C. a sloping channel through which things can descend

D. to descend

1. Which picture shows how <u>slide</u> is used in the sentence below? Fill in the bubble next to your answer.

After the winter storm, Ms Gonzalez was afraid the car would <u>slide</u> down the icy road.

○ A.    ○ B.    ○ C.

2. What does <u>slide</u> mean in the sentence below? Fill in the bubble next to your answer.

It was amazing to watch the snow <u>slide</u> down the mountain during the avalanche.

○ A. to descend

○ B. to coast over ice

○ C. to go unattended

○ D. to glide smoothly

3. For each picture, write a sentence using <u>slide</u> in a way that matches the meaning shown.

_____

_____

_____

_____

_____

4. In which sentence does the word <u>slide</u> mean the same thing as in the sentence below?
Fill in the bubble next to your answer.

> Skip discovered he could <u>slide</u> down the barn's old hay chute by sitting on a burlap sack.

○ A.   The <u>slide</u> at the park is very slippery and usually has a long line.

○ B.   The runner was able to <u>slide</u> into home plate just before being tagged.

○ C.   The workers <u>slide</u> the packages down the chute to the delivery trucks below.

○ D.   Wearing the fuzzy socks, Kate could <u>slide</u> easily across the polished wood floor.

Challenge: Draw It!

Draw a picture with a caption or a cartoon that illustrates how someone could confuse two definitions of the word <u>slide</u>.

To parents   Go to page 113 and do Activity 1 or 3 with your child.

Spare

Spare can mean:

A. a small amount of

B. an extra car wheel and tire

C. to omit or withhold

D. a score in bowling – knocking down all ten pins with two bowls

1. Which picture shows how spare is used in the sentence below?
   Fill in the bubble next to your answer.

   There was a very small serving of spaghetti left over,
   so I had a spare dinner.

   ○ A. 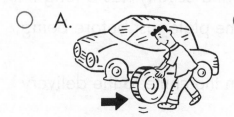   ○ B.    ○ C.

2. What does spare mean in the sentence below?
   Fill in the bubble next to your answer.

   We told Lucy to spare us the boring details and just give us
   the short version of her hospital adventure.

   ○ A. an extra thing or part
   ○ B. small amount of
   ○ C. to omit or withhold
   ○ D. to set aside for a particular use

3. For each picture, write a sentence using <u>spare</u> in a way that matches the meaning shown.

_____

_____

_____

_____

_____

_____

4. In which sentence does the word <u>spare</u> mean the same thing as in the sentence below?
Fill in the bubble next to your answer.

I was relieved to find a <u>spare</u> in the boot.

○ A.   Jake's dad showed him where to find the <u>spare</u> in case he got a flat while he was driving.

○ B.   Kirah cheered when she bowled a <u>spare</u> and won the match against her older brother.

○ C.   The band members asked shoppers to <u>spare</u> some change so they could raise money for new uniforms.

○ D.   The story of the destructive hurricane was so upsetting, Maggie asked Drew to <u>spare</u> her the gory details.

Challenge: Draw It!

Draw a picture with a caption or a cartoon that illustrates how someone could confuse two definitions of the word <u>spare</u>.

To parents   Go to page 113 and do Activity 2 or 3 with your child.

Spread

Spread can mean:

A. to stretch out, open up, or unfurl

B. an abundance of food set out on a table

C. to apply in a thin layer or coating

D. to be fully extended

1. Which picture shows how spread is used in the sentence below?
   Fill in the bubble next to your answer.

   Bev spread the blanket on the ground and set out the food for the picnic.

   ○ A.    ○ B.    ○ C.

2. What does spread mean in the sentence below?
   Fill in the bubble next to your answer.

   When holding a basketball, spread your fingers as much
   as you can for the best grip.

   ○ A.   to push or move apart
   ○ B.   to apply in a thin layer
   ○ C.   to make widely known
   ○ D.   a distribution over time

3. For each picture, write a sentence using <u>spread</u> in a way that matches the meaning shown.

_____

_____

_____

_____

_____

_____

4. In which sentence does the word <u>spread</u> mean the same thing as in the sentence below?
Fill in the bubble next to your answer.

The police officers <u>spread</u> out in the crowd and quickly found the lost little boy.

○ A.   Kevin's grandmother <u>spread</u> an extra blanket on his bed to help him stay warmer.

○ B.   The newspaper club members were excited to see the <u>spread</u> for their first edition.

○ C.   The news of the principal's retirement <u>spread</u> quickly through the school community.

○ D.   Coughing into your elbow when you have a cold can help prevent the <u>spread</u> of germs.

Challenge: **Write It!**

Use the word <u>spread</u> in at least two different ways in a meaningful sentence or short story.

_____

_____

_____

_____

_____

To parents   Go to page 113 and do Activity 1 or 3 with your child.

Suit

Suit can mean:

A. a set of clothing or armor intended to be worn together

B. one of the four sets into which a deck of playing cards is divided

C. to please; satisfy

D. to provide with clothing or armor

1. Which picture shows how <u>suit</u> is used in the sentence below?
   Fill in the bubble next to your answer.

   The coach helped Hanna quickly <u>suit</u> up to substitute for the injured goalie.

   ○ A.    ○ B.    ○ C.

2. What does <u>suit</u> mean in the sentence below?
   Fill in the bubble next to your answer.

   Robert's grandmother adapted the recipe to <u>suit</u> his dietary requirements.

   ○ A.   to meet the needs of

   ○ B.   to provide with armor

   ○ C.   to sue in a court of law

   ○ D.   to adapt or make appropriate

3. For each picture, write a sentence using <u>suit</u> in a way that matches the meaning shown.

_____

_____

_____

_____

_____

4. In which sentence does the word <u>suit</u> mean the same thing as in the sentence below?
Fill in the bubble next to your answer.

> The contractor's sign on the vacant lot that was for sale read "Will Build to <u>Suit</u>."

○ A. My aunt tried to have enough different drinks to <u>suit</u> everyone's liking.

○ B. The <u>suit</u> against the convicted felon is expected to be highlighted on the news.

○ C. The welder had to <u>suit</u> up with protective gear before working on the steel beams.

○ D. Owen had to buy a black <u>suit</u> to wear when he played with the symphony orchestra.

Challenge: Write It!

Write a dialogue between two characters. Each person must use the word <u>suit</u> in a different way in a meaningful conversation.

To parents Go to page 113 and do Activity 3 or 5 with your child.

Sweep

Sweep can mean:

A. to win all games of a series

B. a thorough search of an area

C. to clean a surface with a broom

1. Which picture shows how <u>sweep</u> is used in the sentence below? Fill in the bubble next to your answer.

   After he cleaned the chimney, Leroy had to <u>sweep</u> the fireplace hearth.

   ○ A.    ○ B.    ○ C.

2. What does <u>sweep</u> mean in the sentence below? Fill in the bubble next to your answer.

   After the hockey team's <u>sweep</u> of the championship series, the town had a parade to honor the players.

   ○ A.   a wide curving motion
   ○ B.   an overwhelming victory
   ○ C.   to search an area thoroughly
   ○ D.   to win all the games in series

3. Find the definition of <u>sweep</u> that each person below would most likely use. Write the letter on the line.

_____ housekeeper   _____ firefighter

_____ police   _____ sportscaster

_____ janitor   _____ baseball player

4. In which sentence does the word <u>sweep</u> mean the same thing as in the sentence below?
Fill in the bubble next to your answer.

Alyssa's <u>sweep</u> of her first ping pong championship was unexpected, given her tough competition.

○ A. The umpire called "time" to <u>sweep</u> the dust and dirt off of home plate.

○ B. Sullivan won all five tennis matches of the competition and was credited with a <u>sweep</u>.

○ C. The team could not believe they were able to <u>sweep</u> the playoffs and win all six games.

○ D. The chimney <u>sweep</u> could see the stadium when he went up on the roof to check the flue.

Challenge: Draw It!

Draw a picture with a caption or a cartoon that illustrates how someone could confuse two definitions of the word <u>sweep</u>.

To parents   Go to page 113 and do Activity 3 or 5 with your child.

Switch

Switch can mean:

A. to shift or exchange

B. a moveable section of railroad

C. a device to connect or disconnect an electrical current

D. a thin, flexible twig or stick, especially one used for whipping

1. Which picture shows how <u>switch</u> is used in the sentence below?
Fill in the bubble next to your answer.

The lion tamer used a <u>switch</u> to keep the lion under control during the circus act.

○ A.    ○ B.    ○ C.

2. What does <u>switch</u> mean in the sentence below?
Fill in the bubble next to your answer.

Sofia asked Nancy if they could <u>switch</u> snow cones since she didn't really like grape.

○ A. a whip

○ B. to move

○ C. a change

○ D. to exchange

3. Find the definition of <u>switch</u> that each person below would most likely use. Write the letter on the line.

_____ coach   _____ conductor

_____ power plant operator   _____ fashion model

_____ engineer   _____ backstage crew

_____ electrician   _____ horse-carriage driver

4. In which sentence does the word <u>switch</u> mean the same thing as in the sentence below?
Fill in the bubble next to your answer.

> They had to <u>switch</u> planes in California during their trip from New York to Hawaii.

○ A. The carriage driver used a <u>switch</u> to keep the flies off the horse's back.

○ B. The passengers on the broken bus will <u>switch</u> to a new bus as soon as it arrives.

○ C. The train moved onto the <u>switch</u> so it could transfer to the tracks heading west.

○ D. Matthew asked if could <u>switch</u> books for the project so he could research airplanes.

Challenge: Write It!

Use the word <u>switch</u> in at least two different ways in a meaningful sentence or short story.

To parents Go to page 113 and do Activity 3 or 5 with your child.

Date: _____

Table

Table can mean:

A. a flat-topped piece of furniture

B. a group of people assembled at a table for a meal or game

C. a chart that lists facts and figures

D. suitable for serving for eating or drinking

1. Which picture shows how <u>table</u> is used in the sentence below?
   Fill in the bubble next to your answer.

   The <u>table</u> of guests at the restaurant enjoyed talking
   until the meal was ready.

   ○ A.    ○ B.    ○ C.

2. What does <u>table</u> mean in the sentence below?
   Fill in the bubble next to your answer.

   Mandy bought a big bag of <u>table</u> grapes for the teachers
   to eat at their meeting.

   ○ A. for use on a table
   ○ B. a level area or flat surface
   ○ C. a flat-topped piece of furniture
   ○ D. suitable for eating or drinking

3. Find the definition of <u>table</u> that each person below would most likely use. Write the letter on the line.

_____ waiter

_____ statistician

_____ analyst

_____ carpenter

_____ scientist

_____ board game players

4. In which sentence does the word <u>table</u> mean the same thing as in the sentence below?
Fill in the bubble next to your answer.

The cafeteria <u>table</u> had to be cleaned after the first graders ate tacos for lunch.

○ A. My dad got the card <u>table</u> out for us to work on the 500-piece puzzle.

○ B. The scouts were hoping to hike to the <u>table</u>, or plateau, area by lunch time.

○ C. The lunch monitor created a <u>table</u> to show who got to line up for lunch first each day.

○ D. The <u>table</u> of fifth graders had the cleanest area, so they got to line up first for recess.

Challenge: Write It!

Write a dialogue between two characters. Each person must use the word <u>table</u> in a different way in a meaningful conversation.

To parents Go to page 113 and do Activity 2 or 4 with your child.

105

Vault

Vault can mean:

A. a burial chamber

B. an arched ceiling or roof

C. a secure compartment for valuables

D. a running jump or leap over an obstacle

1. Which picture shows how <u>vault</u> is used in the sentence below?
Fill in the bubble next to your answer.

The architect suggested a barrel <u>vault</u>, or ceiling,
for the atrium in the new bank.

○ A.  ○ B.  ○ C.

2. What does <u>vault</u> mean in the sentence below?
Fill in the bubble next to your answer.

Austin received a perfect score for the <u>vault</u> and won
the final round of the gymnastics competition.

○ A. to jump across or leap over

○ B. a secure, strong compartment

○ C. a running jump over a pommel horse

○ D. to push off and leap over a pommel horse

3. Find the definition of <u>vault</u> that each person below would most likely use. Write the letter on the line.

_____ banker   _____ architect

_____ coroner   _____ pole vaulter

_____ gymnast   _____ security guard

4. In which sentence does the word <u>vault</u> mean the same thing as in the sentence below?
Fill in the bubble next to your answer.

Larry used a stick to help him <u>vault</u> across the stream without getting wet.

- ○ A.   In gym class, we learned how to <u>vault</u> on the pommel horse safely.
- ○ B.   During their basic training, the recruits had to <u>vault</u> over a cement block wall.
- ○ C.   The gymnast had a perfect <u>vault</u> over the pommel horse in the final round of competition.
- ○ D.   Michael's pole <u>vault</u> was high enough to qualify him for the national meet next month.

Challenge: Draw It!

Draw a picture with a caption or a cartoon that illustrates how someone could confuse two definitions of the word <u>vault</u>.

To parents Go to page 113 and do Activity 3 or 5 with your child.

107

Well

Date: _____

> **Well** can mean:
>
> A. in good health
>
> B. a hole drilled into the earth to tap underground water, petroleum, etc
>
> C. a receptacle or reservoir used to contain liquid
>
> D. an enclosed space for receiving and holding something, such as a plane's landing gear

1. Which picture shows how <u>well</u> is used in the sentence below? Fill in the bubble next to your answer.

   The landing gear retracts into the wheel <u>well</u> after an airplane takes off.

   ○ A.    ○ B. 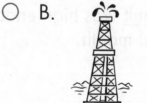   ○ C.

2. What does <u>well</u> mean in the sentence below? Fill in the bubble next to your answer.

   The ink in the <u>well</u> overflowed and made a mess of the paper.

   ○ A. an enclosure for pumps

   ○ B. to rise to the surface

   ○ C. a container for liquid

   ○ D. with care or attention

108

3. For each picture, write a sentence using <u>well</u> in a way that matches the meaning shown.

_____

_____

_____

_____

_____

_____

4. In which sentence does the word <u>well</u> mean the same thing as in the sentence below?
Fill in the bubble next to your answer.

After years of lessons, Sami now dances quite <u>well</u>.

○ A. Josh did not feel <u>well</u> so Mrs Rice sent him to the school nurse.

○ B. After several visits to the hospital, my grandmother was still not <u>well</u>.

○ C. Maggie did very <u>well</u> on her science quiz, which helped bring up her grade.

○ D. After being bullied by older kids, Laura's eyes began to <u>well</u> up with tears.

Challenge: **Write It!**

🖉 Use the word <u>well</u> in at least two different ways in a meaningful sentence or short story.

_____

_____

_____

_____

_____

To parents   Go to page 113 and do Activity 1 or 2 with your child.

Review 3: Guess the Word!

Choose the word that best completes each pair of sentences. Fill in the bubble next to your answer.

1. I got hungry again soon after my _____ lunch.

   I can _____ you the boring details of my trip.

   ○ A. material
   ○ B. run
   ○ C. pocket
   ○ D. spare

2. He charged an exorbitant _____ for his work, given its poor quality.

   Tara's reading _____ improved after three months of fluency practice.

   ○ A. pound
   ○ B. fine
   ○ C. rate
   ○ D. range

3. The chef _____ icing between each of the seven layers of the decadent cake.

   The _____ at the buffet table was impressive.

   ○ A. range
   ○ B. spread
   ○ C. rate
   ○ D. switch

4. The band got together every Saturday to _____.

   The girls couldn't wait to see the _____ that Doug gave Erin when he proposed.

   ○ A. bowl
   ○ B. rock
   ○ C. suit
   ○ D. vault

5. The managers sat at the _____ for the meeting.

   We had to put our results from the experiment in a _____ with clearly labeled rows and columns.

   ○ A. range
   ○ B. pass
   ○ C. spread
   ○ D. table

6. The _____ suspect in the robbery case was arrested by the police.

   For math homework we had to identify all the _____ numbers between 1 and 50.

   - ○ A.   prime
   - ○ B.   spare
   - ○ C.   key
   - ○ D.   mean

7. The students had to find the median, mean, and _____ for each set of numbers.

   Wayne's new kitchen comes with a _____.

   - ○ A.   prime
   - ○ B.   rate
   - ○ C.   pass
   - ○ D.   range

8. Tom asked Ben to _____ places with him.

   Jasper had trouble finding the _____ to turn on the light in the dark room.

   - ○ A.   slide
   - ○ B.   switch
   - ○ C.   sweep
   - ○ D.   suit

9. The farmer was grateful for the _____ that watered the crops.

   Her friends threw her a baby _____ before her son was born.

   - ○ A.   sweep
   - ○ B.   shower
   - ○ C.   judge
   - ○ D.   line

10. Each student in the laboratory was responsible for preparing one _____.

   The cement ran out of the truck, down the _____, and into the new sidewalk frame.

   - ○ A.   slide
   - ○ B.   well
   - ○ C.   rock
   - ○ D.   log

11. Kathy had laryngitis so she had to _____ to the items on the menu she wanted to order.

The radius is the measurement from the center to any _____ on the circumference of the circle.

- ○ A. line
- ○ B. point
- ○ C. pen
- ○ D. place

12. During art class, the students had to _____ clay into mythical creatures.

In order to get into better _____, Brian has been exercising every morning before work.

- ○ A. spread
- ○ B. switch
- ○ C. order
- ○ D. shape

13. The President chose to _____ his power to change the policy.

After her teacher said it was a good brain _____, Tanisha now does lots of Sudoku puzzles.

- ○ A. draft
- ○ B. fix
- ○ C. exercise
- ○ D. hand

14. After students finish their vases, the art teacher will _____ them in the kiln.

The lawyer plans to _____ questions at the defendant, hoping to get a confession.

- ○ A. fire
- ○ B. crash
- ○ C. angle
- ○ D. fix

15. Darnell decided to _____ the change from his lunch rather than give it to his mother.

Emily found the keys in her _____.

- ○ A. patch
- ○ B. pass
- ○ C. material
- ○ D. pocket

Extension Activities

Activity 1: More Meanings

Read some of the other definitions of the word which are not in the grey box from the Dictionary Section on pages 114 to 126. Then challenge your child to come up with sentences using the word in different contexts and with different meanings.

Activity 2: Parts of Speech

Read the sentences on the page. Then ask your child to say if the word is being used as a noun, a verb or an adjective.

Activity 3: Contextual Clues

Reinforce your child's understanding by going through the example sentences again. Ask your child to pick out the clues that helped him to identify the correct definitions.

Activity 4: A Picture Web

Write the word in the center of a large piece of paper. Then have your child search magazines to find pictures that illustrate various meanings of the word. Ask your child to cut and paste those pictures on the paper and write the respective meaning of the word next to the word. Do this for a few different meanings to create a picture web for the word.

Activity 5: Matching Meaning

Prepare two sets of definition cards for different definitions of the word. Play a game of charades or a modified game of Pictionary. Take turns with your child to act out or draw clues while the other tries to guess the meaning of the word.

Dictionary of 50 Words With Multiple Meanings

Angle

noun

- a viewpoint; standpoint
- the place or position from which an object is presented to view
- the figure formed by two lines diverging from a common point

verb

- to set, fix, direct, or adjust
- to turn sharply in a different direction
- to fish with a hook and line

Balance

noun

- an instrument used for weighing
- an equal distribution of weight, amount, and so on
- the remainder or rest
- a physical equilibrium

verb

- to make the necessary entries in an account so that the sums of the two sides will be equal
- to bring to or hold in equilibrium

Boot

noun

- a shoe that extends up all or part of the leg
- the place where the top of a convertible car fits when it's lowered
- a metal device attached to the wheel of a parked car so that it cannot be driven away

verb

- to kick; drive by kicking
- to dismiss or discharge
- to start a computer by loading the operating system

Bowl

noun

- a deep, round dish used for holding liquids, food, and so on
- the contents of a bowl
- a bowl-shaped part, as of a spoon or pipe
- a postseason game played between specially selected college teams

verb

- to participate in a game of ten-pin or duck-pin
- to throw or roll a ball

114

Catch

noun
- a game in which a ball is thrown from one person to another
- a quantity that is caught
- anything that latches, such as a latch on a door

verb
- to seize or capture
- to grab so as to stop the motion of
- to come upon suddenly
- to receive, incur, or contract
- to be in time to get aboard a train, boat, or other vehicle
- to see or attend
- to become lighted

Character

noun
- a personality
- a person with a striking, unusual, or funny personality
- a person in a play or work of fiction
- integrity and force of personality
- a letter of the alphabet
- a written symbol

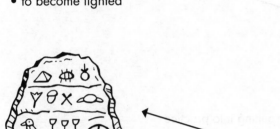

Crash

noun
- a sudden loud noise from something being violently smashed or struck
- a collision of automobiles, trains, or other vehicles
- starched cotton fabric used to reinforce the spine of a bound book
- a sudden failure of a computer program or operating system

verb
- to make a loud, clattering noise
- to break into pieces violently and noisily; shatter
- to collide
- to fall asleep
- to find temporary lodging or shelter, as for the night

Dash

noun
- a small amount; bit
- a hasty or sudden movement; a rush or sudden onset
- the punctuation mark (—) used to show a sudden break in a thought or to set it apart
- a short, fast race
- a quick run or rush
- a dashboard beneath the windshield in a vehicle

verb
- to do hastily
- to destroy or ruin
- to move with sudden speed; rush
- to knock, throw, or smash with violent force

Draft

noun

- a drawing, sketch, or design
- a first form of any writing, subject to revision
- a current of air in any enclosed space
- a selecting of new players from a group of amateur players by professional sports teams
- a preliminary version of a law
- a system for selecting individuals from a group for military service

verb

- to draw up in written form; compose
- to draw the outlines or plan of; sketch
- to take or select by a draft
- to drive or ride close behind another vehicle so as to benefit from the reduction in air pressure

Exercise

noun

- the act of using or putting into practice
- bodily or mental exertion, especially for the sake of training or improvement of health
- a written composition or musical piece executed for practice
- an activity or lesson completed to develop or increase skill
- a traditional ceremony

verb

- to exert muscles in various ways to keep fit
- to make use of one's privileges or powers

Faint

verb

- to collapse and temporarily lose consciousness

adjective

- lacking clarity, loudness, brightness, or strength
- feeling weak and dizzy; about to lose consciousness
- lacking courage; cowardly

Fast

verb

- to give up food for a period of time

adjective

- quick; swift; rapid
- indicating a time in advance of the correct time
- done in comparatively little time
- loyal; devoted

adverb

- quickly, swiftly, or rapidly
- soundly

Fine

noun

• a sum of money imposed as a penalty for an offense

verb

• to charge a financial penalty

adjective

• of superior quality
• consisting of minute particles
• delicate in texture
• healthy; well

adverb

• in an excellent manner
• very small

Fire

noun

• flames that give off light and heat
• something that is burning
• great enthusiasm

verb

• to dismiss from a job
• to inspire someone
• to discharge a weapon
• to set off or launch
• to bake in a kiln
• to utter or ask rapidly

Fix

noun

• a repair, adjustment, or solution, usually of an immediate nature
• a clear determination
• a compulsively sought dose or infusion of something

verb

• to repair or mend
• to stare at an object steadily
• to put in order; adjust or arrange
• to place definitely and permanently
• to arrange the outcome or action of
• to prepare

Hand

noun

• a style of handwriting
• the part of the human body attached to the end of the arm (palm, fingers, and thumb)
• a pointer on a clock or watch
• a round of applause
• assistance or help to do something
• hired help for manual labor; laborer
• a linear measure equal to 4 inches, used in determining the height of horses
• the cards dealt to or held by each player at one time

verb

• to give someone something

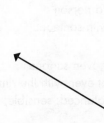

Judge

noun
- a person who selects the winner of a contest
- a court official who decides legal cases
- a person qualified to pass critical judgment

verb
- to rate contestants
- to conclude from evidence
- to make a careful guess about; estimate

Key

noun
- a small metal instrument specially cut to fit into a lock and move its bolt
- something that clarifies a problem
- an explanation of abbreviations and/or symbols used in a dictionary, map, or diagram
- one of a set of levers pressed in operating a typewriter, computer keyboard, calculator, or other mechanical device
- one of the levers in a musical instrument that sets in motion the playing mechanism
- tone or pitch

verb
- to set text in type, using a machine that is operated by a keyboard

adjective
- important; essential; fundamental; pivotal

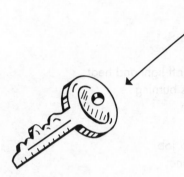

Lap

noun
- the front part of the human body from the waist to the knees when in a sitting position
- a complete circuit of a course or track

verb
- to get a circuit or more ahead of a competitor in racing
- to take in liquid with the tongue
- to move in small waves with a light slapping or splashing sound

Level

noun
- a device used for determining or adjusting something to a horizontal surface
- measure or degree of intensity or achievement
- relative position or rank on a scale
- a story or floor of a building
- a position with respect to a given or specified height

verb
- to make a surface even or flat
- to knock down a person
- to talk frankly with someone

adjective
- having a flat or even surface
- filled to a height even with the rim of a container
- mentally well balanced; sensible; rational

Line

noun

- a phrase or sentence spoken in a play
- a one-dimensional series of connected points in a plane
- a row or series
- people, animals, or things standing one behind the other; queue
- a row of written or printed letters, words, or text on a page
- the wires connecting telephones to one another
- a length of nylon or cord which is attached to a hook for fishing

verb

- to mark with a line or lines
- to form a line or border along
- to cover the inner side or surface of

Log

noun

- a small section of a tree trunk or branch
- a journal or diary
- a record of a machine's performance

verb

- to cut tree branches or trunks into small sections
- to cut down, trim, and haul timber
- to note data or observations into a journal
- to travel for a certain distance or a certain amount of time
- to enter identifying data into a computer system to be able to use it

Match

noun

- a game or contest in which two or more opponents compete
- a pair of like items or people
- a pair of things that go well together
- a small stick from which fire is struck

verb

- to be alike
- to go well with
- to put two things together
- to do as well as
- to put into competition

Material

noun

- the substance of which a thing is made
- cloth or fabric
- the tools needed to make or do something
- a person considered as having qualities suited to a particular activity

adjective

- of, relating to, or in the form of matter
- of or affecting the well-being of the body
- of substantial importance; of much consequence

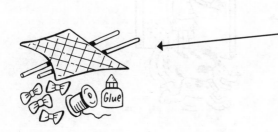

Mean

noun
- the average of a set of numbers

verb
- to intend
- to signify
- to have the importance or value of

adjective
- unkind; nasty; malicious
- bad-tempered
- skillful or impressive
- average of a set of numbers

Order

noun
- an authoritative command or mandate
- succession or sequence
- a request made by a customer for a good or service
- a condition in which everything is as it should be
- proper, satisfactory, or working condition
- conformity or obedience to law or established authority
- a portion of food in a restaurant

verb
- to give a direction or command to
- to make a request for something
- to arrange things one after another

Out

noun
- a play in baseball in which a batter or base runner is retired

verb
- to make known; tell

adjective
- absent, away from
- not functioning, not working
- exposed, visible
- not currently stylish, fashionable, or in vogue
- not available
- external; exterior
- unconscious

adverb
- the opposite of in
- away from the center or middle
- in the open air
- not in the normal or usual place or position
- to a state of depletion or nonexistence

preposition
- used to indicate movement or direction from the inside to the outside of something
- used to indicate movement away from a central point

Pass

noun
- permission to enter
- a free ticket or permit
- the transfer of a ball or puck from one teammate to another

verb
- to allow to go through or beyond a gate or barrier
- to complete successfully
- to go beyond; surpass
- to deliver or transfer
- to sanction or approve
- to throw a ball from one person to another
- to come to or toward, then go beyond
- to skip one's turn in a game
- to qualify for the next level

Patch

noun
- a piece of material placed over a hole to mend it
- a covering for the eye
- a small piece or area
- a small plot or garden
- a small emblem of cloth sewn to one's clothing

verb
- to mend with small pieces of material
- to repair or restore in a hasty or makeshift way

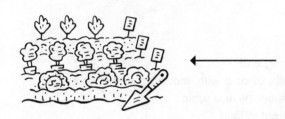

Pen

noun
- a writing instrument with ink
- a person's style or quality of writing
- a small enclosure for animals
- a dock with a protective structure overhead, used to repair submarines
- a female swan

verb
- put down in writing
- to draw with an ink pen
- to confine in a small enclosure

Place

noun
- a particular area of space or spot
- a particular point one has reached
- a seat for one person
- a house or dwelling
- the position in a numeral or series

verb
- to earn a specified standing with relation to others, as in a competition
- to put in a particular position or location
- to rank or put in an order or sequence
- to appoint a person to a job
- to identify in a particular context

Pocket

noun

- a piece of fabric attached to a garment that forms
  a pouch
- a recess in a wall for a sliding door
- a small, isolated, or protected area or group
- any of the pouches at the corners and sides of a
  pool table
- the deepest part of a baseball mitt where the ball is
  usually caught
- a pouch in an animal body, such as the abdominal pouch
  of a kangaroo

verb

- to put into one's pocket
- to conceal or suppress

adjective

- small enough or suitable for carrying in a pocket

Point

noun

- a sharp or tapering end
- a mark made with, or as if with, the sharp end of something
- any definite position, as in a scale
- a particular moment in time
- the important part of a story or joke
- a significant idea or argument
- a unit of scoring or counting
- any place where lines intersect or meet
- a mark used to indicate a decimal

verb

- to indicate position or direction of
- to direct attention to
- to direct or aim
- to have a tendency toward something
- to fill and finish the joints of masonry with cement or mortar

Pound

noun

- a unit of weight
- a monetary unit in various countries
- a place for confining and sheltering stray animals
- a heavy or forcible blow

verb

- to strike repeatedly with great force
- to effect by striking
- to crush by beating repeatedly
- to beat or throb, as the heart

Prime

noun
- a grade or designation indicating the highest quality
- a positive integer that is not evenly divisible by any integer except itself and 1

verb
- to make ready; prepare
- to pour or admit liquid into a pump to expel air and prepare for action
- to cover a surface with a preparatory coat of paint

adjective
- of the greatest relevance or significance
- first-rate
- of the highest U.S. government grade of meat

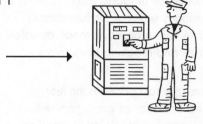

Range

noun
- a large tract of grassy, open land on which livestock can graze
- an amount or extent of variation
- a stove with spaces for cooking a number of things at the same time
- a place to practice shooting at targets
- the difference between the largest and smallest values in a statistical distribution

verb
- to vary within certain limits
- to roam or wander freely
- to have a certain variety of things somehow related
- to be capable of reaching a maximum distance

Rate

noun
- an amount of one thing measured in relation to another
- a price charged on the basis of a standard
- a level of quality
- a degree of speed

verb
- to judge the quality or worth of
- to place in a certain rank or class
- to evaluate the performance of
- to merit or deserve
- to estimate the value of

Rock

noun
- a hard, naturally-formed mineral or stone
- a firm foundation or support
- a large gem, especially a diamond
- a swaying movement

verb
- to sway back and forth gently
- to cause to shake or sway violently
- to upset or unnerve; stun
- to dance to or play rock music

Run

noun

- a hurrying to or from some point
- a line or place in fabric where a series of stitches have come undone
- a continuous series of performances
- the score unit in baseball made by safely running around all the bases and reaching home plate

verb

- to move at a fast pace on the feet
- to creep or climb, as growing vines
- to flow, as a liquid, electricity, and so on
- to spread over a material when exposed to moisture
- to operate or function

Shape

noun

- an outline or contour
- the contour of a person's body
- something, such as a mold, used to give form
- an orderly arrangement

verb

- to give definite form or character to; create
- to direct the course of

Shower

noun

- a brief fall of precipitation
- an abundant flow; an outpouring
- a party held to honor and present gifts to someone for a specific reason
- a bath in which the water is sprayed from overhead
- the stall in which water sprays from overhead

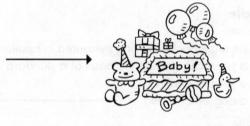

verb

- to pour down in great amounts
- to wash oneself in a shower bath

Slide

noun

- a sloping channel through which things can descend
- a small, flat piece of glass on which specimens are mounted for microscopic study
- the descent of a large mass of earth, rocks, or snow
- a page in a PowerPoint presentation

verb

- to slip or skid
- to glide or pass smoothly
- to hand or slip something easily or quietly
- to go unattended or unacted upon
- to drop down and skid into a base to avoid being tagged out in a baseball game
- to descend

Spare

noun
- an extra thing or part; a replacement
- an extra car wheel and tire
- a score in bowling—knocking down all ten pins with two bowls
- a small amount of

verb
- to save or relieve from an experience or action
- to give up or lend without inconvenience
- to omit or withhold

adjective
- being in excess; more than is needed
- lean or thin
- not being used

Spread

noun
- an expansion, extension, or diffusion
- a cloth covering for a bed
- an abundance of food set out on a table
- a food mixture to be smeared on another food, such as bread
- the two facing pages of a book or publication

verb
- to stretch out, open up, or unfurl
- to distribute over a greater area of space or time
- to apply in a thin layer or coating
- to be fully extended or displayed
- to make or become widely known

Suit

noun
- a set of clothing or armor intended to be worn together
- one of the four sets into which a deck of playing cards is divided
- the process of suing in a court of law; legal prosecution

verb
- to make appropriate, adapt, or accommodate
- to meet the requirements of; fit
- to please; satisfy
- to provide with clothing or armor

Sweep

noun
- a wide, curving motion
- the winning of all stages of a game or contest
- one who sweeps, especially a chimney sweep
- a thorough search of an area or building

verb
- to clean or clear a surface with, or as if with, a broom
- to search an area or building thoroughly
- to win all the games in a series

125

Switch

noun
- the bushy part of the tail on some animals, such as a cow
- a moveable section of railroad track used for diverting moving trains
- a thin, flexible twig or stick, especially one used for whipping
- a shift or change
- a device used to turn on or off electric current

verb
- to move or transfer
- to connect or disconnect an electric circuit
- to shift or exchange

Table

noun
- a flat-topped piece of furniture with one or more leg supports
- a plateau
- a chart that lists facts and figures, usually in columns and rows
- a group of people assembled at a table for a meal or game

verb
- to postpone consideration of

adjective
- of, pertaining to, or for use on a table
- suitable for serving for eating or drinking

Vault

noun
- a secure, strong room or compartment for safekeeping valuables
- an arched ceiling or roof
- a burial chamber
- a running jump over a pommel horse

verb
- to make in the form of an arch
- to jump across or leap over
- to leap over a pommel horse, using the hands for pushing off

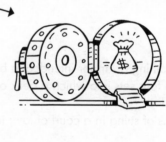

Well

noun
- a hole drilled into the earth to tap underground water, petroleum, etc.
- a receptacle or reservoir used to contain liquid
- an enclosed space for receiving and holding something, such as a plane's landing gear

verb
- to rise to the surface, ready to flow

adjective
- in good health
- satisfactory, pleasing, or good

adverb
- in a good or satisfactory manner
- skillfully or proficiently
- in a comfortable or affluent manner; in financial comfort
- thoroughly, carefully, or soundly

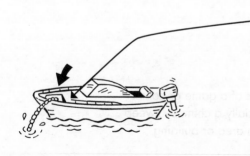

Answer Key

Challenge sections: Answers will vary. Check work for correct use of the word.

Angle: Pages 6–7
1. B   2. B
3. Answers will vary.   4. B

Balance: Pages 8–9
1. C   2. C
3. Answers will vary.   4. A

Boot: Pages 10–11
1. C   2. B
3. C model   A punter
   C cobbler
   B programmer
   A soccer player
   D automobile dealer
4. D

Bowl: Pages 12–13
1. A   2. B
3. Answers will vary.   4. D

Catch: Pages 14–15
1. C   2. C
3. C goalie   A hunter
   D traveler   B carpenter
   A exterminator
   B cabinet maker
   D train conductor
4. A

Character: Pages 16–17
1. A   2. C
3. Answers will vary.   4. C

Crash: Pages 18–19
1. C   2. A
3. Answers will vary.   4. C

Dash: Pages 20–21
1. A   2. A
3. C chef   C baker
   D editor   A courier
   B sprinter   D author
4. B

Draft: Pages 22–23
1. C   2. B
3. Answers will vary.   4. C

Exercise: Pages 24–25
1. B   2. C
3. C pianist   B athlete
   B gym teacher
   A graduate
   B body builder
   C band director
   A army general
4. C

Faint: Pages 26–27
1. A   2. D
3. Answers will vary.   4. D

Fast: Pages 28–29
1. C   2. B
3. Answers will vary.   4. B

Fine: Pages 30–31
1. C   2. B
3. A doctor   D banker
   B jeweler   C hairstylist
   D librarian
   D parking attendant
4. B

Fire: Pages 32–33
1. C   2. A
3. D firefighter   B potter
   A lawyer   B clay artist
   A police officer
   C rocket scientist
   C pyrotechnician
4. D

Fix: Pages 34–35
1. C   2. A
3. Answers will vary.   4. C

Hand: Pages 36–37
1. B   2. C
3. C factory owner   C farmer
   D manicurist   C ship's crew
   B member of a theater audience

   D sign language interpreter
4. B

Review 1: Pages 38–39
1. angle   2. bowl
3. balance   4. crash
5. boot   6. character
7. dash   8. catch
9. faint   10. fast

Judge: Pages 40–41
1. B   2. A
3. Answers will vary.   4. A

Key: Pages 42–43
1. B   2. A
3. Answers will vary.   4. B

Lap: Pages 44–45
1. B   2. D
3. Answers will vary.   4. A

Level: Pages 46–47
1. A   2. D
3. Answers will vary.   4. D

Line: Pages 48–49
1. A   2. C
3. Answers will vary.   4. B

Log: Pages 50–51
1. C   2. D
3. Answers will vary.   4. B

Match: Pages 52–53
1. B   2. C
3. Answers will vary.   4. C

Material: Pages 54–55
1. A   2. A
3. Answers will vary.   4. D

Mean: Pages 56–57
1. B   2. C
3. Answers will vary.   4. D

Order: Pages 58–59
1. B   2. B
3. A coach   D waiter
   C soldier   B sales clerk

A drill sergeant
C security guard
4. C

Out: Pages 60–61
1. A   2. D
3. C boxer   D umpire
   A student   C wrestler
   B repairperson
   D baseball player
4. D

Pass: Pages 62–63
1. C   2. C
3. Answers will vary.   4. A

Patch: Pages 64–65
1. A   2. B
3. D tailor   C scout
   C soldier   A gardener
   D seamstress   A farmer
4. C

Pen: Pages 66–67
1. B   2. B
3. B poet   A artist
   C farmer   C rancher
   B novelist   C shepherd
4. D

Place: Pages 68–69
1. B   2. A
3. Answers will vary.   4. A

Pocket: Pages 70–71
1. C   2. C
3. Answers will vary.   4. C

Review 2: Pages 72–73
1. lap   2. log
3. key   4. level
5. material   6. judge
7. line   8. match
9. mean   10. order

Point: Pages 74–75
1. A   2. B
3. Answers will vary.   4. B

Pound: Pages 76–77
1. A   2. C
3. A grocer   D banker
   A dietician   B carpenter
   D Englishman   C cardiologist
4. D

Prime: Pages 78–79
1. B   2. B
3. A chef   A butcher
   D mechanic   A food inspector
   C mathematician
   C algebra teacher
4. A

Range: Pages 80–81
1. B   2. B
3. D chef   A golfer
   A police   A archer
   D caterer   C statistician
   C mathematician
4. A

Rate: Pages 82–83
1. C   2. A
3. D banker   B babysitter
   C book critic   C contest judge
   A race car driver
   A marathon runner
4. C

Rock: Pages 84–85
1. C   2. A
3. D jeweler   B guitarist
   B musician   D bride-to-be
   A seismologist
   B dancer
4. B

Run: Pages 86–87
1. C   2. B
3. C artist   B plumber
   B electrician   C dry cleaner
   D marathon runner
   C painter
4. C

Shape: Pages 88–89
1. B   2. C
3. Answers will vary.   4. D

Shower: Pages 90–91
1. A   2. B
3. C housekeeper   B bride
   A farmer   C plumber
   A weatherperson
   B expectant mother
4. C

Slide: Pages 92–93
1. C   2. A
3. Answers will vary.   4. C

Spare: Pages 94–95
1. C   2. C
3. Answers will vary.   4. A

Spread: Pages 96–97
1. C   2. A
3. Answers will vary.   4. C

Suit: Pages 98–99
1. B   2. A
3. Answers will vary.   4. A

Sweep: Pages 100–101
1. A   2. D
3. C housekeeper   B police
   C janitor   B firefighter
   A sportscaster
   A baseball player
   D horse-carriage driver
4. B

Switch: Pages 102–103
1. A   2. D
3. A coach
   C power plant operator
   B engineer   C electrician
   B conductor   A fashion model
   A backstage crew
   D horse-carriage driver
4. B

Table: Pages 104–105
1. C   2. D
3. D waiter   C analyst
   C scientist   C statistician
   A carpenter
   B board game players
4. A

Vault: Pages 106–107
1. A   2. C
3. C banker   A coroner
   D gymnast   B architect
   D pole vaulter
   C security guard
4. B

Well: Pages 108–109
1. A   2. C
3. Answers will vary.   4. C

Review 3: Pages 110–112
1. spare   2. rate
3. spread   4. rock
5. table   6. prime
7. range   8. switch
9. shower   10. slide
11. point   12. shape
13. exercise   14. fire
15. pocket